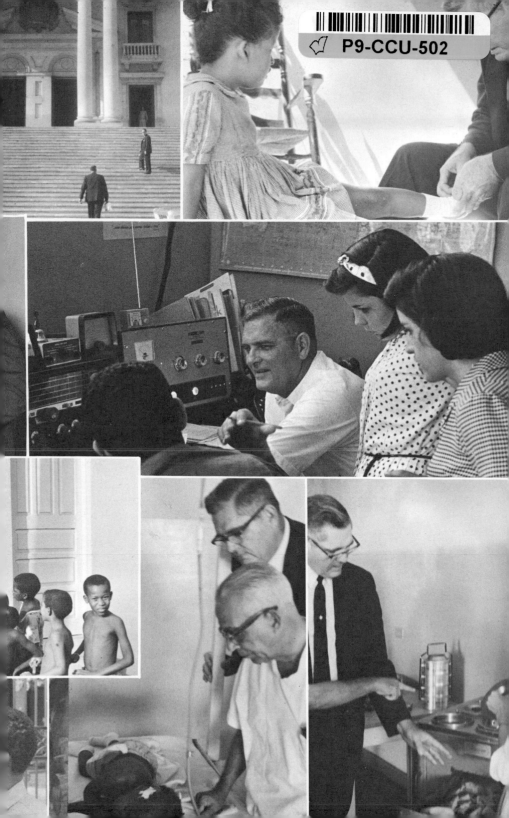

Intrigue
in SANTO DOMINGO

Intrigue
in SANTO DOMINGO

The Story of Howard Shoemake

Missionary to Revolution

by
James C. Hefley

Word Books/Waco, Texas/London, England

To J. Raymond Knighton and his associates in the Medical Assistance Programs' (MAP) office and warehouse, who by unselfish service have helped make this book possible

Contents

"I followed a hard-sell philosophy for ten years as a pastor and fifteen as a missionary. I was obsessed with the idea of staying busy, preaching every Sunday. I mistook religious activity for spirituality. Something happened to change that when I came to the Dominican Republic." H.S.

1

THE REVOLUTIONARY WHO
CAME TO DINNER

As a free-lance writer, I choose people for stories. My specialty is Christianity in life, which is much more important (and interesting!) than what movie stars do with the shades pulled down or the way an ex-shoeshine boy makes a million on the stock market.

This book was started on a bright April morning in church, not where I usually look for good subjects. I find them more often on space pads, in football fields, and in other places where the action is. Anyone can look pious and act godly in church.

Our family was in church together for the first time in six weeks. A great, hulking man stood in the pulpit. Howard Shoemake, I noticed in the bulletin; a missionary to the Dominican Republic.

1

Because there are coming to be more countries than college football teams, I had to think a minute. Suddenly I remembered and nudged my wife. "Hey," I whispered, "remember that young general in officer's school who used to fly Zsa Zsa Gabor around the country when Uncle was dishing out foreign aid money to his dictator father?"

She gave me that can't-you-think-of-better-things-to-talk-about-in-church look and frowned.

"And his sister, Flo something-another, was married seven times. One of her husbands was Porfirio Rubirosa. And the newspapers claimed their father, the dictator, had a college professor killed in New York who criticized his regime. Then the dictator was killed, and three or four years later there was a revolution and the U.S. sent troops in to cool the situation. There was a lot of controversy over that."

She muttered something about little boys who never grow up and talk in church.

"That's the country the speaker is from," I said.

The choir's call to worship cut me off; and after the usual routine that is repeated in thirty thousand Baptist churches every Sunday morning, Howard Shoemake began to talk in a hoarse voice.

He didn't talk about the Trujillos. Mainly he told stories about his missionary work in Colombia and Ecuador, where he served before going to the Dominican Republic. Near the end he got around to the little Caribbean country and the work he had begun there. "The last four years have been the happiest of my twenty years of missionary service," he said. "I've learned to let myself go and relax and enter the doors God opens. He's opened doors to ministries I never dreamed of before. We've been privileged to help save the lives of many children."

The tall man glanced at his watch. I'm one who often nods during any preacher's sermons, but this time I was wide-awake and wanting him to continue.

When the deacon pronounced the benediction, Marty and I looked at each other. "Did you get the feeling that he was hesitant to tell about his new work?" I asked.

She nodded.

"If we could have him out for dinner, we could ask some more questions."

Long ago Marty got accustomed to having last-minute guests; but this time she said, "I was thinking the same thing, but arrangements must already have been made for him by the deacons. Anyway, there's nothing cooked."

I looked at the big man moving toward the vestibule. "Maybe he doesn't have a place to go," I said uncertainly. "We'll wait and see."

We stood near the door and watched our fellow church members file by. It really seemed crazy to wait. Ours is one of those proper suburban churches where guest speakers are treated like visiting royalty.

But this day it happened. The last church member left, and Howard Shoemake was left looking for his dinner hosts. "That must be us," I said and introduced my wife and three daughters. "There must have been a mixup; so if you don't mind speedy fried chicken from a shopping center franchise, come with us."

He didn't mind, so off we went for the unplanned dinner.

Later both our pastor and a deacon were much embarrassed. Each thought the other had made arrangements. They vowed that it would never happen again and apologized for the inconvenience. But events proved to us that the mixup was providential and most convenient.

After sixteen pieces of chicken we moved to the family room. Cindy, ten—our oldest—plumped a globe on the missionary's long legs and said, "Show us your country."

He ran a long finger southwesterly from the tip of Florida, across the narrow coast of Cuba and the Windward Passage, stopping at the ragged-edged island of Hispaniola that lies midway along the curving chain of islands called the West Indies. "My country shares this big island with Haiti. It is a beautiful land of palmed beaches, green mountains, and rich valleys. Columbus loved it better than any other place he visited in the new world. Columbus is buried here in Santo Domingo."

Our six-year-old Cecilia also knew about Columbus and stood intrigued as the missionary continued: "Columbus' brother, Bartolome, founded Santo Domingo and named it for the patron saint of their father, St. Dominic. Later the French settled in the western third of the island and called their colony Saint-Domingue. This is now Haiti, where French is still spoken. Spanish is spoken in the eastern two thirds, which since 1821 has been the Dominican Republic.

He was warming up.

"There's more history in Santo Domingo than you can imagine. It was the first European city in the New World. Here was the first European university, the first Catholic cathedral and first monastery, the first mint for manufacturing coins, and even the first Masonic lodge in the Americas."

Howard looked at our two school-age daughters. "The Dominican Republic is the only country in the world with the Bible in its flag. It has red and blue squares separated by a white cross with the open Bible in the center with a laurel branch on one side and a palm branch on the other. The laurel stands for immortality and triumph, and the palm symbolizes liberty. Tradition says that the Bible is open at John 8:32: 'Ye shall know the truth, and the truth shall make you free.' The first Catholic missionaries in the Americas came to Santo Domingo in 1496. They beat Southern Baptists by 466 years. We're really Johnny-come-lately's."

I thought our guest must be tired. He sounded hoarse. I learned he had spoken earlier in the morning to an Episcopalian congregation. He was hoarse from scar tissue that followed three tonsillectomies. "I'm getting my sec-

When leaving Dominican shores, Columbus is said to have remarked, "There lies the land of God." His statue stands in front of the National Cathedral, the oldest in the New World. His remains (bottom) are inside the Cathedral. *Below:* The Dominican flag is said to have the Bible open at John 8:32.

ond wind," he insisted. "I enjoy telling you about our country. Not enough North Americans are interested."

Not thinking of anything better to say, I ventured, "How have the Dominicans responded to Baptist missionary work?"

He grimaced. "I was afraid you would ask that. But I'll level with you. We have two small chapels that will shortly be organized into churches. About twenty members in each. Our third missionary couple is opening work in Santiago, the second largest city. A fourth couple is coming from language school."

I'm the usual North American, quick to measure success by statistics. Forty members in five years. I estimated more than $50,000 of Baptist mission money had been spent, not counting the time of the Shoemakes and the newer missionaries. Recalling the much publicized U.S. foreign aid to the Trujillo regime, I began to suspect the country must be a sinkhole. (Later I saw this exact description—a "sinkhole"—applied to the country by a *Look* magazine editor.) I understood why Howard Shoemake had not mentioned mission figures in his sermon.

"Uh, I suppose the revolution hurt your work," I said. "It sure created a lot of fuss in this country."

A pained look crossed his face as if I had reopened an old wound. "The Dominican civil war was tragic—awful tragic. But it gave us the greatest opportunity to serve we've ever known."

He stopped and remained silent. I hesitated to probe further. This was like asking a war veteran about the horrors of war.

Then I recalled his mentioning in his sermon medical work with children. "Tell us about the medical work. What are you doing?"

The steel-blue eyes set in his poker face suddenly flashed. "Sixty percent of the deaths every year are children under five. The biggest killer is gastrointestinal diseases. You have to see it to believe it. More cases die in a day in this tiny country from these diseases than the average U.S. doctor sees in a lifetime. Dr. C. Everett Koop from Philadelphia and some others came down. We took a survey. Tramped the streets and countryside until our feet were sore. We saw them dying. We found a way to help."

The dam had burst. Howard Shoemake was off and running. Marty whispered, "Get your tape recorder." Remembering past-due assignments, I hesitated. "You'll regret it if you don't," she said.

I got the recorder, and for three more hours Howard Shoemake talked. About the children of the Dominican Republic. About four Dominican medical doctors whom, as he said, "the Lord gave us." About the bloody revolution and the fear-filled nights when refugees had packed his house. Then we snacked and went back to church and saw his slide pictures of the land Columbus "loved most."

He left for Texas and the final months of his furlough with his family. I went to the big closet in my study that is lined with shelves holding back issues of about thirty different magazines. I scanned several months of *Time* reports on the Dominican revolution. I found other material about the dramatic U.S. intervention that had rocked the world. Suddenly a sentence stood out—a quote from a U.S. diplomat on the scene during the months of violence following the initial battles: *"Howard Shoemake, a U.S. Baptist missionary, is the most influential foreigner in the Dominican Republic."*

U.S. diplomats do not have a reputation for making such statements about missionaries. The sparks that had been glowing since the preceding Sunday afternoon exploded into a blaze. I felt that the story of Howard Shoemake, missionary to revolution, must be written.

I called a man in Wheaton, Illinois, whom Howard had mentioned. Ray Knighton, executive director of Medical Assistance Programs, had visited the Dominican Republic. He knew Howard Shoemake well and what he had done. "You're stepping into a controversial situation here," he said bluntly. "I think Howard did what a missionary should do under these situations. But not all evangelical Christians will agree."

There's nothing that whets a writer's interest more than to hear that a subject is controversial. (I have about decided that only controversial people get things done.) I listened to the tapes and shot off a proposal to a book publisher. A not-sure-this-will-sell answer came back. I queried Word Books. Their answer was much more encouraging. Word would pay an advance and expenses to the D.R.—the familiar initials which Howard had used for the country. I wrote back, "Send your contract."

I left on another assignment enroute to Mexico City via Miami and the Southern Baptist Convention before the contract came. In Miami I saw Howard Shoemake again. This time he was wearing a telephone booth. After extricating his 6'5", 260-pound frame from the booth, he explained briefly that he had been ironing out the diplomatic ruffles in arranging for a Dominican girl heart patient to return to the U.S. for a postoperative checkup.

I met green-eyed Dorothy Dell, only seven inches shorter than Howard, stately with delicate light gray hair and looking as a Southern lady should. "She's the celebrity this week," Howard said proudly.

She was indeed. Dorothy Dell (friends use both names) captivated the Woman's Missionary Union meeting in Miami Beach Auditorium with an account of their service during the revolution. She and a Cuban missionary shared the same program with messages on the topic, "A Loaf or Coat in His Name."

As the microphones pitched her soft voice over the mammoth auditorium, she recalled ". . . the vivid memory of Sunday morning awaking to the 'thud,' 'thud,' 'thud' of heavy soldiers' feet marching, then running for shelter as the planes flew low over the housetops. . . . the street filled with a mob of people beating the car of an anti-

Communist newsman, then setting it afire . . . our house filling with refugees looking for a safe place to stay.

". . . For eighteen years we had been in Latin America. We had seen governments rise and fall, mob violence and revolutions begin and cease. Usually things were back to normal in a few days, so we expected to 'weather this storm.' . . . But this was not the usual political upheaval. All the ingredients for a civil war were present, plus the possibility of Communist intervention.

". . . Little did we realize how the Lord would use this experience to teach us to 'care' enough to really be able to share 'in His name' with our friends . . . hungry, homeless, and desolate. . . . God opened the hearts of people who were surprised that the missionary would identify himself with them and their human needs, rather than seek safety for himself."

A few blocks away film producer Gregory Walcott was premiering *The Bill Wallace Story* for Convention delegates. Bill Wallace had disdained safety for himself when Mao Tse Tung's Communist armies engulfed his hospital. Dying of unknown causes in prison, Dr. Wallace became the first Southern Baptist martyr to the Communists. As I pushed through the crowd of preachers leaving the theater, many faces wet with tears, I compared Bill Wallace to Howard Shoemake. Both men had been motivated to heal both body and spirit. Both had continued to minister in the midst of violence. But in God's providence one had died and the other lived.

The book contract caught up with me in Mexico City. Before signing it, I wrote Howard Shoemake—who had since returned to Santo Domingo—to request his cooperation.

". . . A book about the work we have attempted to do had been the furthest thing from our minds," he replied. "We have managed to avoid photographers and writers when possible. [I had wondered why he had been mentioned only once in news stories I had read.] There is nothing spectacular about us or our work. Nevertheless, after taking this to the Lord many times in prayer and always feeling that your work will bring glory to the Lord and His work, we have decided to cooperate."

He attached a long list of names with U.S. addresses: "People you may want to interview who know about our work. Most are not Southern Baptists, but may have a few good or bad things to say about our work."

I scanned the locations and occupations . . . Washington, New York, Fort Bragg, Miami, Dallas, Oklahoma City, Chicago. Doctors, ham radio operators, diplomats, soldiers, a Dominican ex-security chief, and the Dominican ex-president who had been forced out during the revolution. At this time it seemed odd that only one was described by Howard as a Southern Baptist. Later this did not seem strange at all when I discovered Howard Shoemake's capacity to make friends of all political and religious stripes.

I asked my travel agency to work out a schedule. It would be wise, I felt, to talk with these people before going to the D.R.

"We must lose our religiosity, pull our robes off, and pitch in to help people. We've got to be servants. We must stop trying to do everything for the glory of Baptists." H.S.

2

FRIENDS IN FOGGY BOTTOM

We purposely live near Chicago's O'Hare, the busiest airport in the world, with jets thicker than blackbirds in a berry patch. It's noisy but convenient. My desk is two hours from Washington.

Friday, September 29. American Airlines Flight to Washington's National Airport. First stop, United States Information Agency (USIA) at 1750 Pennsylvania Avenue, a few blocks from the Department of State building.

Malcolm McClean, special assistant to the deputy director of USIA, had been U.S. Public Affairs officer during the Dominican revolution. A stocky blond man with an athletic build, he was accustomed to being interviewed. He saw quickly what I was after.

"Howard. Yeah, who didn't know him? He was board president of the school our kids attended. Ran a one-man

11

rescue squad during the revolution. Handled hurricanes
and special medical cases with his ham radio."

McClean adjusted his polka-dotted bow tie, then continued. "This is bringing back old memories.

"That revolution was bad, but could have been worse.
Our government was criticized for its intervention, but
we saved a lot of lives, provided food and medical services,
and held the fabric of Dominican society together." He
leaned back in his chair and looked solemn. "I'll never
forget that day at the Embajador—that's the biggest
hotel in Santo Domingo. Hundreds of people were outside
awaiting evacuation when the shooting started. They
were ducking under cars, behind trees, anywhere to escape
the flying bullets. I felt like Gary Cooper. Fortunately,
I knew people on all sides. I got to the leader of the rebel
faction and made arrangements for some buses to take
them to the docks where we were evacuating."

The USIA man paused again and scratched his head.
"I don't recall seeing the Shoemakes at the hotel. I think
they went out a day later. But he came right back at the
ambassador's request. Howard isn't the kind to stay away
from danger when he knows he's needed. He has a special
ingredient in his personality. *Concern* is the word. He
really shows concern for people. And he's completely
apolitical. You should stress that point. All you have to
do is get mixed up in politics in a country like the Dominican Republic and you lose your effectiveness as a missionary."

"Give me a story," I asked.

Malcolm McClean though a moment. "This isn't about
Howard, but maybe it illustrates something. I went with
some rebel soldiers to hurry up the buses. I was in the
front seat with a rebel who was driving my car. Two
rebels were in the back seat. Each had a rifle sticking
out a window. Suddenly one of them asked the driver to
stop. 'What for?' he asked. The soldier said, 'I'm left-
handed and he's right-handed. We need to be in the right

positions to fire.' So the driver stopped and let them change."

McClean leaned back and laughed heartily. "There were a lot of people trying to get in the right position during all the confusion down there. A notable exception was Howard Shoemake. He was in a position to serve everybody."

"Mr. McClean," his secretary interrupted. "Time for your meeting."

I thanked him and McClean said, "We're discussing the controversy over the Vietnam elections. Please excuse me."

"Good luck," I said and left for Foggy Bottom.

The U.S. State Department building is a mammoth, many-caverned complex of offices. The "Foggy Bottom" caricature comes from its pass-the-buck reputation where both Congressmen and newsmen claim difficulties in learning State's position on foreign policy matters.[1] In a building where you need a map to find your way around, the epithet has a second application.

George Brown, a Texas native, now handles State's Dominican desk. He was staff assistant to Ambassador W. Tapley Bennett, Jr., during the Dominican crisis. He interrupted a telephone conversation and greeted me cordially. An oversized map of the Dominican Republic hung behind his desk. He turned back to the phone. "Investment risks are not so great now that the country has calmed down," I heard him say. This and other talk indicated that he was talking with a businessman interested in the D.R.

"Sure, we all remember Howard Shoemake," he said to me a few minutes later. "He was a leading figure of the American community, the model example of a good citizen. His credentials as a good Samaritan were recog-

---

[1] For the record the State Department, through the Secretary of State, acts as the President's principal adviser on foreign policy and has primary responsibility for initiating and implementing foreign policies.

nized by everybody. Anything he wanted from us, he got.

"What did he do? What didn't he do for all of us? With his ham radio he kept us in touch with our families during the crisis. He did things for our Carol Morgan School that no one else could do. But what really stood out to me was the way he helped some Dominican children get special medical help in the United States. Maybe that's because I've got a four-year old myself. I remember this little boy who needed open heart surgery. Howard collected money from Dominican friends and our embassy wives for his family's plane fare. Then he arranged for a ham friend in Boston to meet the boy and his parents and take them to the hospital. The logistics were really complicated. But Howard did it."

"A boy, you say," I broke in. "I thought it was a girl."

George Brown laughed. "That was another case. Where Howard finds these children is a mystery to me. He has a knack for finding them and getting people to help."

"Hey," he said. "I just thought of someone who can help you. Jack Nepple is in his office now. He knows a lot about Howard. He was with AID (Agency for International Development) in the D.R. during the trouble."

Brown escorted me to Nepple's office. Nepple, a little man with a V-shaped hairline, and a veteran AID officer, had served in Cuba both before and after Castro.

"Certainly I remember Howard," he said. "None of us will ever forget him. He did a lot of favors for a lot of people. Especially during the early days of the crisis when there was so much confusion. He was one of the few people willing to go into embattled areas of the old city. He'd take his personal car and load it up with food supplies and medicine and away he'd go while the bullets were flying. Sometimes I doubted if he was going to come back alive."

George Brown interrupted. "In my view he more than carried out a missionary's role during that kind of situation."

The AID man asked, "George, why weren't there any newspaper stories about Howard? I can't recall ever seeing one."

"I guess," the State man said, "that no reporter was enterprising enough to look him up for a story."

"My understanding," I said, "is that he ran from publicity." I laughed. "He's not what Texans are supposed to be."

Brown looked quizzical. "Is Howard a Texan? I'm from Texas myself, but I didn't know that. He never told me."

After leaving the State Department, I phoned the Pablo Gonzales [2] residence. "You are doing a book about Meester Shoemake," a heavily accented woman's voice said. "Come and have dinner with us and we will tell you about him. A wonderful man, that Meester Shoemake. Is the best embassy the United States has in our country. He knows no poor, no rich, no ugly, no pretty, no religion. He's helping for everybody."

When I hung up I blinked in amazement. The name Shoemake was getting to be magic.

An hour later my taxi stopped before a modest red brick house in a beautiful wooded area near Catholic University. The Gonzaleses and their twenty-two-year-old daughter Miranda greeted me as an old friend. Miranda, a bilingual secretary, spoke excellent English, having lived in Washington for six years.

As Mrs. Gonzales served the meal, it was obvious that she was a fish out of water in the kitchen. A bit of biography showed why. Until coming to Washington about a year before, she had enjoyed servants. Mr. Gonzales had operated a mercantile business and also a farm before the revolution. The business was disrupted, the farm infested with bandits. They had come to the

---

[2] I am using assumed names for some Dominicans whose remarks might bring recriminations. Trujilloistas and other extremists are reported still to have power to strike back in some places.

United States to be closer to their daughter and son, a student at a midwestern university.

Did they remember Trujillo?

"Yes," Miranda said in a soft voice, glancing around as if she were still afraid. "I was in school when news came that he was killed. None of us smiled, because we were so afraid. We had never dared make jokes about the dictator. But after we realized almost everybody was against him, we started smiling." She dropped her voice and whispered, "My uncle was killed by Trujillo."

And did they suffer during the revolution?

"How can I describe it?" Mrs. Gonzales said in her awkward English. "It was like, uh—you have seen the movie, *Dr. Zhivago?*"

I nodded.

"That it was like. The stores, the banks, everything was closed. Much killing there was. We are not politicians, just citizens. Our children were in the United States. We could not call them. A friend take us to Meester Shoemake's house. He say, 'Don't worry. Come in and we will pray.' We are Catholic. He is Baptist. He kneeled us down beside his bed and we talk to God. I feel better. My heart had great faith. Then, Meester Shoemake, he help us talk to the children through his radio set. Wonderful, that Meester Shoemake."

Mrs. Gonzales wiped at the stream of tears that had started flowing.

"Soon our food, it was almost gone. 'Pablo,' I say to my husband, 'We must find food.' We start out, but the rebels, they stop us and make us get out of our car. They point their guns. Then one man, he say, 'Don't hurt, that is Pablo Gonzales. I know him. A good man, he is. Pablo,' he say, 'I'm sorry, but there is no food for you.'

"We come to have only one meal left—enough for one person. Pablo and I, we say we will invite Meester Shoemake to eat this meal. He come and we were surprised. That wonderful Meester Shoemake, he bring a big bag of oil, flour, rice, beans, and milk. We feast together. Then he come again with more food. Because of him we did not starve."

I thanked the Gonzales family and rose to leave. "When you see Meester Shoemake," Pablo Gonzales said, "ask him about the rats. He is one big rat killer, him."

The Howard Shoemake story was getting better all the time, and I hadn't even reached Santo Domingo yet.

I stopped next at a high-rise apartment building on the New Jersey side of the Hudson River. The Penick Gentrys. "Bud to my friends," the schoolman said. "Anybody who knows Howard Shoemake is a friend of ours."

Bud Gentry, a school principal by profession, had been principal of the Carol Morgan School in Santo Domingo during the revolution. "I'm now on a contract with the International Schools Service to recruit personnel for 126 overseas schools," he explained. "Carol Morgan is one of these, an English-speaking school for children of some Dominicans, U.S. citizens, and other foreigners. Since Howard was president of the school board, we worked together closely."

"What did you accomplish?" I asked.

"Better give Howard the credit. We got a new high school plant and upgraded the curricula and teaching staff. And except for the first days of the revolution we kept the school open when all other schools in Santo Domingo were closed.

"That man, Howard," Bud Gentry declared, "almost made Baptists out of two Methodists. He didn't do much preaching, but he gave us a lot of example and counsel. One of my secretaries told me Howard had helped her more than all of her pastors ever had.

"Everybody trusted him. He could do things the rest of us couldn't. He helped our new teachers get their clothes through customs without paying duty. He got the fire trucks to bring us water when our school reservoir ran dry. More than anybody else, he was responsible for

getting sixteen acres of land and about $300,000 from the
State Department for a new high school."

Janie Gentry came out of the kitchen with coffee and
rolls ."Did he have opposition?" I ventured.

Bud Gentry gulped his coffee and appeared hesitant to
answer. "Go ahead and tell him," Janie said. "He'll find
out anyway."

"Yes, he had some opposition from other Protestant
missionaries. When you get to the D.R., you'll find out
why."

I went next to the New York financial district and an
office in the aggressive brokerage house of Donaldson,
Lufkin and Jenrette. Gustavo Tavares is a new member
of the firm. Graduate of Brown University and businessman in Santo Domingo. A member of one of the D.R.'s
most famous families.

Tavares drew on his black cigar and reminisced. "My
ancestral roots go back more than five generations in the
Dominican Republic. Howard Shoemake did more for the
Dominican people in four years than any other foreigner
has done in a lifetime."

Tavares mentioned some of Howard's contributions I
had heard from others—medicine, heroic service during
the revolution—and some I had not heard. "He was primarily responsible for getting Dominicans to set up a
warning system on hurricanes and other natural disasters.
He helped the Santo Domingo Chamber of Commerce set
up a business college for training office workers. And the
rats," he added. "Howard may have saved Santo Domingo from a plague with that project.

"Too many foreigners live apart from Dominicans," he
continued. "Howard isn't like that. He is one of the
community; you could almost say he is a Dominican. He
thinks of our problems as his problems."

The Dominican swiveled in his deep chair and frowned.
"Howard came to a developing country that was trying
to have a democratic system after a dictatorship of thirty

years. He realized this and didn't try to change things overnight. He didn't expect too much of Dominicans. He realized that change would come in due time. When the revolution came, many lost faith that our country would survive. But Howard didn't. He always felt we would pull through."

Tavares blew a ring of smoke into the air. "I got to know Howard pretty well. But one thing surprised me. I'm a Catholic. He's a Baptist minister. He never tried to change me. Perhaps he has a different approach than some Baptists. He seldom mentioned his religious organization. We never discussed religion. I just took him for the good friend he was."

From New York I flew to Oklahoma City. Dr. Martin Andrews and his wife Phillis met me at Will Rogers Airport. Dr. Andrews, a Free Methodist physician, had helped Howard set up the medical program to save Dominican children suffering from gastroentritis. He and his wife Phillis had visited the D.R. shortly before the revolution. He looked much younger than his forty-two years.

"I've been in medicine almost fifteen years," he said, "and never imagined such an infant health problem could exist so close to the United States. Thousands of babies were dehydrating and dying until Howard got help. Here was a country with only one school of nursing until Howard helped the Free Methodists and Catholics get one started. There were only about eighty R.N.'s in the whole country. With no health education, the young mothers had no idea of the importance of boiling water and washing hands."

Phillis Andrews broke in. "It was awful." Her smooth face wrinkled as she spoke. "We went on a trip with Howard and the minister of health and saw those babies."

"We saw President Donald Reid Cabral just before he was forced out of office," Dr. Andrews continued. "Everybody at the palace insisted he was too busy talking with generals and politicians. But he wasn't too busy to see Howard."

"I'll never forget that meeting," Mrs. Andrews declared. "The hall was bristling with armed guards. When I opened the door to go to the rest room, two guards leaped to attention. I was so surprised I came to attention myself. Then they escorted me to the door of the rest room."

"You could feel the tenseness in the air as we drove about Santo Domingo," Dr. Andrews noted. "Everywhere we went, Howard knew people. They'd stop him on the street and give him a Latin hug.

"What a relief to get out of the country. Two weeks after we left, the revolution erupted, with the Shoemake family right in the middle of the trouble!"

Phillis Andrews tugged at my sleeve. "While we were there, I had the only two nightmares I've ever had in my life. I've never been the same since. I say to people, 'If you don't want to get involved with suffering people, don't go to a country like the Dominican Republic.'"

Three more appointments were on tap before going to the D.R. I felt a creeping sensation while reflecting upon Phillis Andrews' words: "If you don't want to get involved, don't go." I wondered: How much could a writer get involved in a country and still remain objective? As the plane winged above a mass of dark clouds, I grabbed a news magazine to relax. It was a special issue about "The Permissive Society." After reading *Newsweek's* comparison of United States society to ancient Babylon and to Sodom and Gomorrah, I felt the D.R. could not be much worse.

Major (Chaplain) Arthur Bell met me at the Hendersonville, North Carolina, airport. We drove to Fort Bragg. "This is the home of the 82nd Airborne," he said proudly. "Here you'll find the real patriotic army trooper. These men are all volunteers. They are sent where big trouble breaks out."

We drove by a squad of uniformed men loading duty bags on a truck. "On their way to Vietnam," Art Bell said. "Some of these fellows were probably in the Dominican Republic with Howard."

Art was a Southern Baptist. "I'm glad to find Howard has one friend in his denomination," I said jokingly. "So far I've talked only to Methodists and Catholics."

The chaplain laughed. "I can testify that he's got an army of friends around here. Say, there's Sergeant Miller. He'll remember Howard."

John Miller, a veteran cook, grinned widely when the chaplain said I was going to write a book about Howard. "I think the world of the Reverend," he said. "So do hundreds of other guys who were down there during the trouble. How many calls did he make for us on that ham radio, Chaplain?"

Art Bell smiled. "Way over a thousand, I'd say."

"He made some for me, Chaplain. You're writing a book about Shoemake, huh? Well, look, I've been serving chow to army grumblers for seventeen years, and I've met none better." He winked at the chaplain. "Pardon me for forgetting you, sir."

"Tell him about the cookouts," Art Bell urged.

"Those were great. We had 'em every month. One night I cooked steaks for the ambassador. Cooked for hundreds of the guys, too. We brought our own meat. The guys didn't dare gripe about the food. I had 'em buffaloed. Told them, 'Look, you jerks, we're going to Reverend Shoemake's house, and if I hear even one of you complain, I'll . . .'" The mess sergeant stopped in mid-sentence as he realized the chaplain was within earshot.

"You're going to write something about Reverend Shoemake and us, you say. Well, put something in about the cookouts. I always say the mess hall is the most important part of the Army. I've been saying that for seventeen years. I've . . ."

"Thanks, Sergeant Miller," the chaplain interrupted.

We drove around the sprawling military complex, largest of its kind in the United States. Between visits with soldiers who had served in the D.R., Major Bell spoke his own impressions into my tape recorder. "I'm from a service family," he noted. "My father was in for twenty-one years. I've been a chaplain since 1958. We've been around a lot of missionaries. Howard Shoemake is one of a kind. He never asked any favors of the military when we were in the D.R.—not even mail service or PX items which many civilians, including missionaries, bug us about. No, wait a minute, He did ask us to move several tons of medicine from the San Isidro Air Base to his church. The reason was he couldn't do it any other way."

He reeled off example after example of Howard Shoemake's ministry to U.S. soldiers. "The GIs really needed a friend during that time," he said. "They knew about the critics at home who charged us with intervening for nothing. They felt unappreciated. Howard became sort of their father and pastor away from home. They could use his radio and call home. They could talk to him about personal problems. The commanders appreciated him so much that they held a parade in his honor and awarded him a commendation. And yet they knew Howard was on good terms with the rebels who were shooting at our troops."

"Howard and his family must have sacrificed a great deal," I said.

"They did," the chaplain agreed. "They acted out of love as opportunities arose."

"Mission is where you are," I mused.

"I agree. That's what Howard Shoemake believes."

From Fort Bragg I flew south to Miami, where two Dominicans recalled Howard Shoemake from different perspectives.

"I was director of internal security when the revolution came," suave Tomas Cortinas explained in flawless English. "Before that I was director of communications.

The country didn't need a security department during the revolution since no one could control anything. I resigned."

Cortinas talked with me in his combination office and radio shack where he operates an export-import business.

"After the fighting started I brought my family out on the first plane. Then I went back. It wasn't safe for me to go into the rebel zone—Howard wouldn't let anybody go with him. The rebels escorted him, even though they knew he was helping their enemies."

He looked at his ham set. "That Howard is a good ham operator, too. Hams from all over the hemisphere know him. I've been a ham since 1949, except for a year when the Trujillo government put me off the air. I'm proud to say I helped Howard set up his radio and taught him how to use his set. That man, I tell you, was born special. He is an institution in my country. He made a better name for the Americans than any American I've ever known, and I'm fifty years old."

Cortinas sighed and went on. "I'll have to be honest and say that Howard is a better Dominican than many of my people. He gets them to helping each other. They trust him when they don't trust one another. He makes them feel ashamed that a foreigner has to do what he does. And something else. Howard isn't one who works only for his church's benefit, as most of the priests and reverends in my country do. He works to help the people. Maybe that's what makes him different."

The second Miami interview came in the suburb of Coral Gables where I talked to ex-President Donald Reid Cabral in the study of his U-shaped yellow ranch house. Writers who covered the Dominican Revolution generally held him to be an honest, well-intentioned businessman who served as an appointed president during a difficult time. His efforts to weed out corruption among elements of the military had triggered the initial revolt.

"The last complete history of my country was written

about 1910," the ex-president said as he sat in his shirt
sleeves. He pointed to a wall of books. "I've got everything there that's been written about my country. I want
to write a history myself, but I can't finish it until I can
return to my country and check every statement."

"The events of your country's past are both fascinating
and heart-breaking," I said.

He sighed and brushed a manicured hand through thin-
ning dark hair.

"True. We were the first country to be settled in the
New World. The Spanish couldn't find gold, so they began
leaving for Mexico, Cuba, Venezuela. The population
went down so fast a law had to be passed forbidding people to leave the country. Next came the pirates—Sir
Francis Drake plundered the city and stabled his horses
in the great cathedral. Then in 1795 the French took
Santo Domingo in the Treaty of Basle.

"The slaves in the western third of the island [Haiti]
revolted, and Napoleon sent an expedition to regain control of the whole island. But the Spanish people in Santo
Domingo rebelled and defeated the French in 1809. Spain
held control until 1821, when the people proclaimed the
independence of our 'Great Colombia.'

"But the Haitian army moved in and occupied our
territory until three Dominican patriot leaders made independence a fact and dedicated the Dominican Republic
to 'God, Fatherland, and Liberty.' That was February
27, 1844, a date we Dominicans will never forget."

The ex-president's patriotism showed in his flashing
eyes as he ran on. "The Haitians kept our country in
turmoil. The Dominican government asked to become an
American protectorate in 1869. The U.S. Senate turned
this down by ten votes. One revolution after another followed until in 1916 President Wilson sent Marines to
restore order.

"We were preparing for free elections in 1930 when
Trujillo seized power in a military coup and began his

long despotic rule. As you know, Trujillo was assassinated in 1961. A provisional seven-man council of state guided the country until Dr. Juan Bosch was elected. Seven months later Bosch was ousted by a coup and the powers of state given to a civil junta of three civilians. I was a member of the junta and subsequently became the *de facto* president of the country." He stopped to drink a glass of water. I let the tape recorder run, waiting for him to continue.

"I really tried to help my countrymen. I started with land distribution. Because of Trujillo's greedy policies, the Dominican government then owned a higher percentage of national acreage than any other non-Communist country. The program called for giving land to ten thousand families in one year. In one day we placed fifteen hundred families. I began diversifying agriculture to break the hold which sugar cane had upon us. I started an industrial program to produce steel bars from scrap metal and planned other industries. Then the military forced me out of office."

"From what I know," I said, "you were very fortunate to escape with your life."

"Perhaps. But I was not always worrying about my life. I wanted to show the Dominicans that the country had changed and the old days of assassinations had ended. So, except for official functions, I always drove my own car without a guard and without bullet-proof glass. I took my family to mass and other places as any other private citizen would."

The ex-President looked at me and smiled. "Please forgive me for talking so much about myself. You come to interview me about Howard Shoemake. He was the first Protestant minister I ever knew. He came to see about the medical aid program. He prayed with me. I ordered the departments of government to give him all the help needed.

"You probably know better than I all the good he has

Donald Reid Cabral, ex-president of the Dominican Republic, was interviewed in his Miami home. He spoke of his beginning to diversify agriculture, here represented by the crop of sesame about to be harvested. Dominican economy has traditionally been determined by the sugar cane crop and the world price of sugar.

done," the ex-president continued. "But to me his greatest success was the rehydration program that saved hundreds of babies every year. To save lives, that is the greatest benefit to any country.

"With men like Howard, my country is moving ahead. Even with all that has happened lately, the country is still a lot better than it used to be."

Donald Reid Cabral leaned toward me and thumped the coffee table with his right hand. "No matter what Castro does to disturb the peace, there will be progress. If we had twenty more men like Howard Shoemake, there would be more progress."

We talked an hour longer about the problems in his country. I felt he was sincere, honest, well intentioned, as other writers had said. He walked with me to my Hertz Ford, leaned against the trunk, and talked some more. "One day," he said, "things will get better. I will return to my country and finish my history."

I drove away toward the International Airport. With good connections in San Juan, I would be in Santo Domingo that night.

"We are here as guests of our Dominican friends. We try to look for the good instead of the bad. We think of our being here as an opportunity to serve, not as a job that God and our mission board has forced upon us." H.S.

3

"THE LAND OF GOD"

The Delta 707 jet hummed over the blue Caribbean. From thirty-one thousand feet the Bahamas looked like humped green turtles floating on a ruffled lake. Over to the left I could see tiny San Salvador, on which the Spaniards had first set foot in the New World.

From six miles up I visualized the island shapes as peaks of submerged sea mountains. In the dim past the Caribbean mountains may have stood high enough to have been connected as a continuous land extending to Florida.

The pilot announced we were flying along the northern coast of the Dominican Republic and would soon be landing in San Juan, Puerto Rico. The disjointed mountains on the far right seemed higher and steeper, which they are. Mount Duarte rises over ten thousand feet and is the highest in the West Indies. These peaks are so steep that elevations above three thousand feet are practically uninhabitable.

We landed in sultry San Juan, and the plane disgorged its tourists that had been packed like sardines. I hurried a porter through the throng and into the main terminal to catch my connecting Caribair 5:00 P.M. flight for Santo Domingo. I needn't have hurried. The little Convair puddle jumper did not leave until 7:30 with its trickle of passengers—two or three businessmen, an American baseball player's wife going to join her husband playing winter ball in Santo Domingo, a U.S. AID diplomat, an upper-class Dominican girl returning home from college, and me. The tourists had departed for the glamor spots and health resorts which did not have the reputation of the D.R. for revolutions.

An hour later the plane landed at the Santo Domingo airport. Inside the terminal I hit a snag when the customs officer saw my tape recorder. He pointed to the tape under the glass cover and slowly shook his head. He evidently believed the tape held a propaganda message. I looked plaintively at the man.

A long shadow fell over us. I turned to see Howard Shoemake and joyfully grasped his big hand. He quickly recognized the problem and motioned over the chief inspector. At a word from Howard, the chief handed the recorder to me and smiled his ok.

"You're getting by easy," Howard drawled in his customary hoarse voice. "They say that when Trujillo ran the country he had hidden demagnetizers and X-ray machines to take care of tapes and film going through customs. Come on over and meet my kids. Dorothy Dell is waiting at home."

Taking a bag, Howard pushed ahead of me. He towered at least a foot above the Dominicans around him. Outside the customs gate I met the three youngest Shoemakes. Jimmy, sixteen, was heavy-set and the image of

his father. Ricky, thirteen and thinner, boasted freckles
that seemed to pop with mischief. Twinkle-eyed Carol,
twelve, was already taller than some of the Dominican
ticket girls. Two older boys, Glenn and David, were in
the United States. Glenn was a sophomore at Houston
Baptist College in Texas.

Howard strode through the terminal ahead of us, waving to Dominicans as he passed them. Then we were
packed into his white 1965 Rambler station wagon and
moving out of the parking lot.

We sped alongside the rocky beach which was dotted
with swaying coconut palms. In the pale moonlight I
noticed how the exposed roots of the palms imposed a
touch of ugliness to the scene.

"The Dominicans have carried away the sand," Howard
said, "leaving the palms vulnerable to the next hurricane.
So many don't know how to take care of their natural
resources. You can understand them when you realize
they're just proving their freedom. Under Trujillo it was
illegal to cut down a tree anywhere."

I said, "I guess no one will ever forget Trujillo."

Howard stared straight ahead and did not speak for a
long moment. "I hope you won't talk too much about
Trujillo in the book," he finally said. "I'm glad I didn't
live here when he was in power. I'd rather not have the
memories or have to answer questions. The Dominicans
would like to forget him, but they can't."

I waited, hoping he would go on.

"I'm glad I wasn't here right after he was killed,"
Howard begun, then stopped talking again.

I finally spoke. "Didn't the Trujillo family try to take
over the country?"

"Yes, that's what I've heard and read," Howard replied. "Joaquin Balaguer—who is now the president for
the second time—became president after the dictator's
death. He had been both vice-president and presider during the Trujillo era. Supposedly he was doing a good,

honest job. Trujillo's son, Ramifis, and two brothers plotted to get rid of Balaguer and apparently killed many suspected Trujillo enemies. President Kennedy learned about their plot and sent a fleet of warships into Dominican waters. The Marines were to go ashore if Balaguer needed them. That evidently caused the uncles—the son had already left—to throw in the sponge and leave the country. Kennedy became a hero to the Dominicans for this maneuver. When the Dominicans heard about his death, they flocked to the U.S. Embassy to sign a memorial book. Many wept openly."

"Then you came at a time when Dominicans thought well of Americans."

"I came at God's time," Howard said quietly. I detected the reverence in his voice. "Dominicans thought well of Americans then and they do now. As individuals, I mean. Dominicans differ among themselves on both America's foreign policy and their own politics. But they're the friendliest people you'll ever meet. You'll see."

We left the beach and moved into a populated area. "We're coming into Ozama," Jimmy said. "It's a suburb just across the Ozama River from the main town. Columbus sailed his ships past the spot where we'll cross on a bridge." He added proudly, "Columbus called this country 'the land of God.'"

About ten minutes later we started across the high Duarte bridge, named for the patriot Juan Pablo Duarte, one of the three leaders who had won independence from the Haitians in 1844.[1]

I noticed a giant black spot on one of the high girders. "That's where a rocket hit during the revolution," Howard said. "See those shacks over to the right and down near the river? Every time there's a hurricane we

---

[1] Duarte, along with Francisco del Rosario Sanchez and Ramon Mella, make up the Trinitaria honored at the Dominican national shrine which stands today in Parque Independencia at the head of Calle Conde, the main business street of Santo Domingo. At this spot the patriots proclaimed the Republic's freedom.

have to go down and warn them to get out to safety."

We reached the end of the bridge, went around a traffic circle, and turned into Amado Garcia Street. "You probably saw this street on television a lot during the revolution," Howard said. "The U.S. soldiers opened it up as a corridor between the San Isidro Air Base where they landed and the U.S. embassy. They put down barbed wire at every intersection of streets coming into it."

I looked warily at knots of men gathered on street corners in the warm evening. Hordes of children, most of them ragged and dirty, played in front of shop windows protected by bars. Peering up, I could see families sitting on little balconies.

I commented on the scene and Howard said, "It wasn't much different when the fighting was taking place. People sat in doorways and on balconies and watched as if a carnival were going on."

Armed policemen stood every block or so. I noticed that instead of sidearms, each held a rifle in a ready position. "They just put on twelve hundred new policemen," Howard said. "A lot of other people carry guns; less now, however, than when I came. Guns disgust me."

He turned the wheel of the Rambler to the right. "We'll see the old part of town tomorrow. That's where the rebel stronghold was and where my church is. It's safe to go there now."

We reached a residential area where the houses were better and the streets worse. "These potholes haven't been fixed since the revolution," Howard said. "The government just doesn't have the money."

Suddenly he swung down a smooth, wide street and wheeled into a half-circle drive beside a stucco house. "This is home. Come in and meet Dorothy Dell and we'll have a bite to eat."

Dorothy Dell greeted us at the door. Two dogs, Superman and Topsy, came dashing from the patio to leap on the children. I looked around at the enormous living room, at least thirty-five feet long, I guessed. At one end, backed up against a curtained wall, was Howard's ham radio equipment. Shelves of books, mostly theological and medical, covered an adjoining wall. Several medals and framed awards brightened the opposite wall. The far section of the living room, past the main entrance, looked more conventional with sofa, armchairs, television, and tables.

The house itself was H-shaped, with the connecting living room in the middle, three bedrooms on one spur, and dining room, kitchen, and maid's quarters on the other. A brick-floored patio graced with tropical shrubs and flowers complemented the back area between kitchen and bedrooms.

We moved to a long table in the dining room where I faced a painting of a snow-capped mountain peak. "That's *Mount Chiveborazo* in the Andes," Dorothy Dell said. "We look at that and get homesick for Ecuador."

The maids arrived with cake and coffee. The oldest, Milagros (meaning "Miracles," Dorothy Dell explained), was full-time. The younger, Digna, only fifteen, came from a poor family and attended school during the day. The Shoemakes gave her a home and pocket money. Both girls had come to live with the Shoemakes since their recent return from furlough and had already made professions of faith in Howard's church.

"Goodness," Dorothy Dell went on, "You'd better be careful what you say in the book about our having maids. Every time we go home we have to explain why. Help is cheap here and a necessity if I am to help Howard. Canned goods and frozen dinners are twice as high here as in the States. Meals take twice as much time to prepare."

Howard looked up. "Besides, we get to know another class of Dominicans better this way."

I smiled. "Yes, I've heard about the way you missionaries live in luxury. Such sacrifice! Seriously, though, I understand and will try to make a point in the book."

Howard began riffling through a clip of phone messages. A nun, a doctor, a secretary from the Dominican Department of Health, a U.S. AID technician, and a Mennonite missionary had called. I laughed when he finished reading off the list and said, "What, no Baptist deacon?"

Howard looked at me strangely, seeming unsure of what to say. Finally he said, "My job is to be in touch with people, and few people here are Baptists."

"I didn't intend to be critical," I ventured, "but I've been in the homes of other Baptist foreign missionaries; and they had maids, but they didn't get calls from nuns."

Howard took a long swallow of coffee and leaned back, his face toward the painting of the Andean mountain. "There was a time when I didn't have time for people other than Baptists or potential converts. But God changed that."

"Has the role of the missionary changed?"

"I'm not qualified to speak for every missionary, but the role of this missionary definitely changed."

"When did this happen?"

He closed his eyes. "It isn't that easy to pinpoint. Maybe God started working on me the last year we were in Eucador. But I didn't get His message until after I came here on my survey trip. To understand just how much God has changed my work, you'd have to know what I was before."

"Tell me about yourself," I asked and he did, with Dorothy Dell filling in spots where his memory was weak.

"Before becoming a missionary, I had been a pastor for ten years—the go-go-go type," he said, "who had to preach somewhere every Sunday after God got hold of me at an assembly.

"I was sixteen when I went with my buddy, Udell Smith, to the Baptist camp just across the state line in Louisiana. My family lived then in Port Arthur, Texas, where Dad was chief customs inspector. Well, at the camp I got into some mischief, and they were about to

Howard Shoemake was raised in Port Arthur, Texas, the son of the chief customs inspector. *Top:* Howard stands with an arm around a cousin. *Center:* The Shoemake children as they appeared about 10 years ago: Carol, Ricky, Jimmy, Glenn, David. *Bottom:* Howard and Dorothy Dell with the two oldest sons during their first year of missionary service in Colombia.

Howard and Dorothy Dell served 13 years in Colombia and Ecuador as "church builders." They also helped distribute CARE food commodities and did some medical work.

ship me back home when the night watchman pleaded
for me to be given another chance. The next day God
got hold of me while Dr. Baker James Cauthen was
speaking. He was then pastor of Polytechnic Baptist
Church in Fort Worth, Texas, and professor of missions
at Southwestern Baptist Seminary.[2] Both Udell and I
surrendered to preach. He's now director of student work
for the Louisiana Baptist Convention.

"After that I buttonholed everybody I knew in camp
about surrendering to the Lord. I went home, preached
my first sermon to three people in a mission, and didn't
miss a Sunday preaching for the next ten years. I probably had some influence on my younger brother, Earl.
He went to the seminary and is now a pastor in Columbia,
South Carolina."

Howard said that he met Dorothy Dell at Howard
Payne College, where she was a popular student leader,
secretary of the Texas Baptist Student Union Council,
and in the first group of "Invincibles"—Baptist students
who worked summers in churchless communities.

They married on December 29, 1940, and moved into a
windowless, unfinished house during a snowstorm. The
next summer, after graduation, they moved to Fort
Worth, where the late Dr. L. R. Scarborough appointed
Howard student director of seminary missions at Southwestern Baptist Theological Seminary. He became responsible for some hundred services each week on street
corners and in institutions that ranged from jails to old
folks' homes. "At the seminary," Howard noted, "I felt I
was missing something if I didn't preach at least once
every night. I believe now that I mistook activity for
spirituality."

Midway through seminary he dropped out to become
pastor of the First Baptist Church of Navasota, Texas, a
town of about five thousand. "I did all the promotional

things Baptist preachers are supposed to do," he said.
"The church grew, but I got restless and began thinking
I should do more.

"One morning Dr. Cauthen—by this time he had become a missionary to China—spoke in a special missionary service for my church. Being a customs inspector's
kid who hung around the docks and foreign ships, I had
always been interested in other countries and cultures,"
he said. "Both Dorothy Dell and I grew up in south
Texas, where there are a lot of Tex-Mex people. This
gave us a strong interest in Latin America, although the
only Spanish thing I can remember from high school days
is the song, 'La Cucaracha.' Before high school, I remember that my Junior department in Sunday School bought
a car fender for Miss Essie Fuller, a Southern Baptist missionary to Brazil. So even before Dr. Cauthen came,
Dorothy Dell and I had been thinking about missions
in Latin America. His sermon made us think a little
harder.

"We started exchanging letters with the Foreign Mission Board. We went back to seminary and applied for
appointment. We intended going to Peru, but because of
visa trouble, after language studies we went to Barran-
quilla, Colombia, where I directed the construction of the
Baptist hospital. After three and one-half years in Colombia and a furlough, we transferred to Ecuador and
pioneered Baptist work in the city of Guayaquil."

The maid came with fresh coffee. "I was mainly a
church starter and builder in Guayaquil. At one time I
had twelve mission chapels going. After we left, the
Ecuadorians named a church after us. We protested but
they did it anyway."

Howard paused and shrugged his huge shoulders. "Now
I don't say I did wrong. I think I followed God's guidance
as nearly as I knew how then. But during our last year in
Ecuador the Gospel Missionary Union—that's a 'faith
mission'—asked me to help with their stewardship pro-

gram. I really enjoyed this and started thinking that maybe I had limited myself too much to Baptists, that maybe I had fenced myself in and been too busy to become involved with missionaries and Ecuadorians not in the Baptist camp."

I looked around. The children had gone to bed. Dorothy Dell was nodding. I insisted that it would not be discourteous for her to leave us; and she, too, went off to bed.

Howard continued.

"That year, 1961, I went home for surgery. While recuperating at the Baylor Medical Center, I began feeling that we ought to pioneer somewhere else. So I asked Dr. Frank K. Means, the Foreign Mission Board's secretary for Latin Ameria—he had been my confidant and missions professor at Southwestern Seminary—if the Board knew of a place where the trees weren't cut and the stumps weren't pulled. The Board later sent me to survey the Dominican Republic. I had to look for it on the map. I had always thought the D. R. was in Central America.

"So I came on my survey in February, 1962, and something happened that had a lot to do with getting me to extend my vision."

He paused and looked at his watch. "Ten-thirty. I'm like most preachers—long-winded—but I'll try to hurry up. The airline lost my baggage, leaving me with only the clothes I had on. I had planned to start right away on a survey trip into the back country and look for the best places to establish new churches. But with no clothes—"

"Couldn't you buy clothes in Santo Domingo?" I interrupted.

Howard stood up and stretched his arms. "Look at me. I have a 17½" neck, 37 sleeve, and 50 extra-long coat. They don't sell clothes for elephants down here."

"You had to stay in your hotel?"

"Right. And you can imagine how embarrassing it was

to send my clothes out to be cleaned. I called the desk and they sent a bell boy. I undressed to my shorts, drapped a bed sheet around myself, handed the clothes around the door then waited until the clothes were returned clean.

"After a few days I think just about everybody in the hotel knew about my predicament. It helped in making friends with people.

"In this situation I had to stay in Santo Domingo. After only a few days in this distressing circumstance, the desk clerk called me one evening and said that the director of immigration, Senor Almonsor Veras, wanted to meet me in the hotel lobby at seven the next morning. I was there. Senor Veras greeted me cordially and said, 'I understand you are here to explore the possibilities of getting a permit to live in our country. Forget it—you already have it.' Then he sent me to a notary who happened to be the son of the president. This man didn't know me from Adam but offered to sign for me himself. They ended up asking me only to sign a simple statement pledging not to become a liability.

"This friendliness made me feel wanted. I went around to some more government offices, while the airlines kept looking for my baggage, and met the same cordial treatment. One man said, 'We need all the help we can get. Our country is like a child that has lost a very bad father. We are struggling to build a nation.'

"I picked up a lot of information about the country. Sit here, and I'll get some notes."

I sat and sipped cold coffee for about five minutes while Howard rummaged in the file. Suddenly he shouted, "Here they are! My filing system is awful, but I found them."

He came back with a sheaf of faded notes. I followed his finger as he showed me his survey findings:

People: No color line. Composite of many nationalities and races—Spanish, French, English, African Negroes,

Syrian, small groups of Chinese and European Jews. Lighter-skinned people tend to be in the upper classes.

Economy: At standstill with 35 percent or more unemployed. Drained by Trujillo family, which may have taken more than half billion from country. Per capita annual income $218. Typical wages: bank clerks—35¢ per hour; miners—30¢ per hour; farm workers—20¢ per hour.

Education: 50 percent of adult population illiterate. Only 25 percent of school-age population attending elementary schools. Only 8 percent of these complete elementary grades. Only 2 percent of the 8 percent finish high school. Only 20 percent of the teachers high school graduates.

Health: Only 63 percent of urban population receiving water service. Worse in rural areas. Greatest reported cause of death: gastroentritis originating from poor sanitation and health practices. Infant mortality 135 per 1000 before the first year. Annual population increase— 3.5 percent. Only 80 registered nurses for 11,400 beds.

Information outlets: 80 radio stations, 30 of which are in Santo Domingo. One Government-operated television station with relays for distant cities. One small commercial television station reaching only Santo Domingo.

Religion: Roman Catholicism "official religion," but religious toleration for all beliefs. Site of many important Catholic "firsts" in the New World: first Catholic mass (1493); first Catholic see (1511); first archbishopric (1547); first cathedral (1541). Ecclesiastical structure developed for Santo Domingo, the first Spanish colony in the New World, became the model for the rest of Spanish America. Country now 92-95 percent Catholic; 2 percent Protestant; about 1,000 Jews and the rest none or other religions. Catholic figures almost certainly misleading, in view of situation in other Latin countries.

Howard shoved the notes toward me. I put them in my attache case for later reference. "I know it's late," I said, "and I'm tired, but tell me about the rest of your survey."

"I went back to the hotel and wondered what a missionary should do, if anything, about some of these needs. The airline still hadn't found my baggage, so I looked up some evangelical missionaries in the capital. Statistics were hard to come by even from them, but I managed to formulate some information I knew my Board would want.

"The first Protestant missionary had been S. E. Mills in 1889, who worked for eighteen years as an independent missionary before affiliating with the Free Methodists. The Free Methodists and the Seventh Day Adventists were strong on education and church building. About a dozen other missions had emphasized church building. Somehow they all seemed to have managed to survive under Trujillo. One told me, 'We minded our own business and stayed out of politics. The dictator didn't bother us.' I tallied up what numbers I could get. The largest was the Dominican Evangelical Church with about thirty thousand members. It came from a merger of the Methodists, Presbyterians, Moravians, and Church of the Brethren. The Assembly of God, the Free Methodists, and the Adventists were next in size, but none half as large as the Evangelical Church."

"No Baptists?" I asked.

"Oh, yes, there were some Baptists. Independent Baptist missionaries started work in 1949, but had only four small churches in the country when I came. You can talk to Bob Meyers about how their work is going now. Be better if you get your information from him."

Howard leaned back and yawned. "Pan Am finally found my baggage after cabling every one of their offices in the Caribbean. It was at the other end of the island in Port au Prince, Haiti."

I yawned, too.

"We'd better get on the hoss and get you to bed," Howard said. "Your room is across the street."

I followed Howard directly across the street to a yellow brick residence. A large sign in English had been painted over the entrance: FIRST BAPTIST CHURCH. "The English-speaking church is renting it for services," he said. "You'll have a good air-conditioned room all by yourself." When he noticed that I looked nervously up and down the street, he added, "You'll be in no danger. There have been quite a few burglaries around lately. But no violence."

In my room I enjoyed a hot bath and got ready for bed. Then I remembered what Mrs. Gonzales had said in Washington: "Our revolution was like *Dr. Zhivago*." I fished the book out of a bag and tried to concentrate before falling asleep.

"Most of my Dominican friends are not evangelicals. Many probably will never join my church. But they are still good, loyal friends. To me a friend is not somebody who always agrees with me, nor someone who doesn't see my faults. He is someone who defends me at my back and is loyal when I need him." H.S.

4

A PECULIAR MISSIONARY

The "early bird" is not yet a satellite to the Dominicans. The rooster's shrill crowing awoke me at daybreak. The air conditioner had stopped working, and there was no water in the bathroom. I soon learned that hardly anything works by American standards in the Dominican Republic, even in Santo Domingo, a city of 450,000 population. "You should have been here during the revolution," several people told me.

I dressed and sat down to think a bit about the month of research that lay ahead. In correspondence Howard had said he hoped I would do an objective story which wouldn't be all piety and flowers. This had been my desire, too. I have had a growing feeling that too many "Christian" books are marred by a lack of realism. Sacred cows are kept tethered behind high fences of silence.

Characters talk in the clichés of Zion. Catholics and cock-
tails, to cite two examples, are usually handled negatively.

The Shoemake story didn't seem to call for a straight
biography. After all, I felt (as I frankly told Howard
later) that Howard's boyhood, his Texas pastorates, and
even his thirteen years of missionary service in Ecuador
and Colombia were not extraordinarily interesting. The
distinctiveness of his service seemed to center in the D.R.
There seemed to be a story worth telling in his mission to
revolution, his departure from conventional missionary
work, his Christian humanism.

With razor and toothbrush in hand, I walked out into
the fresh November morning. Cars, mostly foreign makes
(an American compact costs $6,000 in the D.R. with
duty), were racing by at 50 to 60 miles per hour. Later I
learned there are no speed limits in Santo Domingo and
only one traffic light.

The Shoemakes were gathering for breakfast when I
came in exclaiming about the traffic. Howard read a devotional from Acts 13:44-52 about the Jews' envy over
the multitude of Gentiles that came to hear Paul. He
prayed that "we will not permit jealousy and envy of the
success of other Christian workers to hinder our work."

The children began talking about a threatened long-
shoreman strike, wondering if President Balaguer was
going to permit them to march to the palace. "If he does,
there'll be trouble," Jimmy said. To which Ricky added,
"Hooray, maybe we'll get out of school!"

"Speaking of school, you boys had better get moving,"
Dorothy Dell reminded.

"I take them," Howard said aside to me. "Carol goes to
the old Carol Morgan School building. A neighbor takes
her with his girl, and we pick them up. The boys go to
the new high school that Bud Gentry probably told you
about. Come along with me and you'll see part of the
city. When we get back, I'll make a phone patch to a
nun in Chicago."

We loaded into the car, with Ricky lagging behind. "C'mon, boy, get on the hoss," Howard scolded. "You'll be late for your own funeral."

He drove south toward the seacoast for about two miles and then turned west. "Up ahead is the home of General Antonio Imbert. He is one of the two men still living out of the twenty said to have been involved in the killing of Trujillo. He was also one of the many who governed awhile during the revolution. See the soldiers in their station out in front of the house? He'll need armed guards as long as he lives."

Acting on a foolish impulse, I raised my camera for a picture. The soldier instantly reached for his gun. I dropped the camera back into my lap.

All Howard said was, "Better watch how you take pictures around here. The guard probably thought you were drawing a gun." I said nothing, concealing my surprise at Howard's calm reaction.

We drove through a section of new houses into the fringe of the city. Here the houses were only shacks. A line of five girls, each balancing a five-gallon water can on her head, faced us as we turned a curve. "There's a faucet down the road," Howard said. "The whole neighborhood gets its water there."

We reached the new Carol Morgan High School, a modern one-story brick building covering about a half acre. A line of cars were discharging children of various colors. "Good school?" I asked Jimmy.

"Sure is," he replied. "When we went home on furlough last year, we found we were ahead of the kids in Fort Worth."

"The mini-skirts are already in down here," I said to Howard as the boys got out.

Howard laughed. "That's the way you tell the American and European girls. The Dominican girls are more modest."

Looking above the milling students, I saw the Domini-

In this slum
(below) in down-
town Santo
Domingo, 2000
people share one
water pump and
one stool.
Right: Children
balance five-
gallon water cans
on their heads
going to and
from a pump.

can and American flags flying in the stiff breeze from the Caribbean only a few hundred yards away. "We're all proud of this school down here," Howard said. "It means that we can keep our children with us and know they are getting quality education. But it didn't come easy."

I remembered what people had told me back in the States. Later I intended asking Howard about his work as president of the school board.

We were passing the shacks when I clicked on the recorder and thought of something I might have missed the night before. "You said the lost baggage kept you in Santo Domingo on your survey trip. Didn't you get into the country towns after you got your baggage back?"

"Oh, I didn't tell you that. Yes, I did. A missionary friend took me in his car. I paid for the gas. This gave us an opportunity to get better acquainted and to understand one another's motives."

"How extensive was this survey?"

"There's a map in the glove compartment. You can understand better if you follow along with it.

"We started from Santo Domingo—"

"But," I interrupted, "it's Ciudad Trujillo on this map."

"I picked that map up at a service station. I'm surprised they're still using it. They've destroyed just about everything else with his name on it. He named it City of Trujillo after himself right after he got into power. When he was killed the government changed it back to Santo Domingo, the name given by Columbus' brother.

"Anyway, we first drove westerly along the coast to San Cristobal. That's Trujillo's hometown and the city where the first constitution of the country was signed. We drove on to Azua, which as you see is almost on the ocean. That's a very old town, founded about ten years after Columbus came. Cortez, Pizarro, and Balboa all lived there before taking off on their history-making expeditions.

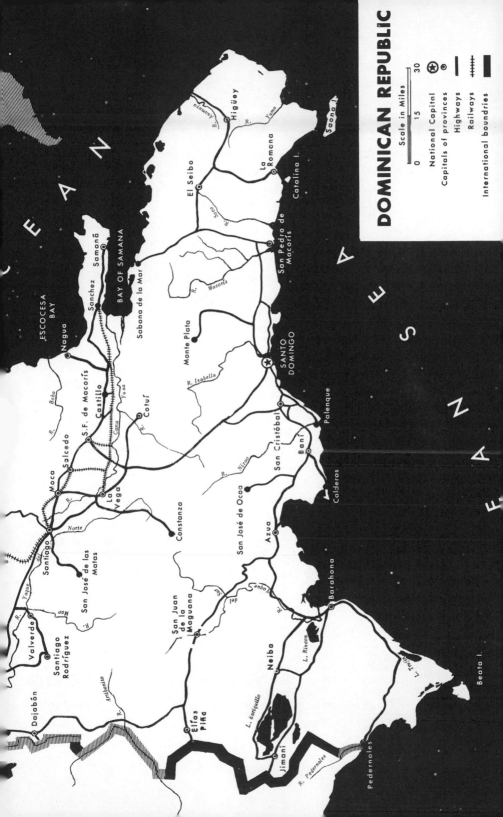

"We turned northwesterly and inland a little way from Azua and drove into the narrow San Juan Valley, where the high mountain walls are something to see. Look just north of the town of San Juan de la Maguana and you'll see Santiago, the second largest city in the country. San Juan and Santiago are only about fifty-five miles apart through the mountains, but the road isn't always passable. You can go on west and circle down along the Haitian border, then come back to Santiago. But that road isn't always safe either. We circled back by Santo Domingo. Then we took the Duarte Highway to La Vega, which is only about thirty miles from Santiago. On a later trip I went to Santiago; this is where the Free Methodists have a twelve-grade school and where one of our newer Southern Baptist missionary couples now have a good work going.

"We drove into La Vega, which is the market center for the richest valley in the country. People are very conservative there and loyal to the Catholic Church. Near La Vega the Spaniards defeated the native Taino [1] Indians in a decisive battle. Legend has it that Columbus' men won by divine intervention. The Catholic Church is building a big shrine there which some Catholics say is a waste of money that could be used for the poor.

"From La Vega we drove to some northern towns—Moca, Salcedo, and San Francisco de Macoris. Then we came back to Santo Domingo. The country isn't very big, as you can see by the map."

"How did you feel about the prospects for Baptist mission work?" I asked.

---

[1] In 1492 an estimated one million Taino Indians roamed the country they called *Quisqueya*. Peaceable by nature, they probably came from a fiercer tribe on the northern coast of the South American continent. After the Spaniards arrived the Tainos died off rapidly from exhaustion, starvation, disease, and other causes. By 1548 the Taino population was down to about five hundred. To replace Indian workers, the Spaniards began importing Negro slaves from Africa. Today the Taino chieftain Enriquillo, who resisted the Spaniards, is a Dominican hero. The word *Quisqueya* stirs patriotic fervor, and the national anthem begins *"Quisqueyanos valientes."*

"I felt we had a great opportunity here; every town of five or ten thousand or more had one or more small struggling evangelical churches of some kind. But the missionaries I talked to admitted they weren't touching the great masses of people. I felt that a good corps of missionary preachers and money for buildings could put us in every population center within ten years. I didn't meet one unfriendly Dominican. The door seemed to be wide open. I made some very optimistic projections to the Foreign Mission Board."

"Such as . . ."

"I suggested that the first missionary couple begin in Santo Domingo and buy radio and TV time and newspaper space to present our doctrines to the Dominicans. They could also do personal work and direct home Bible studies to build up a nucleus for starting a chapel about six months after arrival. Future missionaries, I felt, could start preaching missions in Santo Domingo and other cities. By 1965, I estimated Southern Baptists could be ready to start a theological institute in the capital or in Santiago. By 1967 I suggested we might move into elementary and secondary schools. I had some big ideas, boy, some mighty big ideas. Fortunately or unfortunately, depending on how one looks at mission work, it hasn't all panned out this way."

Howard turned north into a broad avenue. A stream of students were crossing in front of us. Noting the buildings and banners I assumed this was the Autonomous University of Santo Domingo (*Universidad Autonimade Santo Domingo*) and said so.

Howard slowed the car. "You're right. This is the oldest [2] university in the Western Hemisphere, although the first is in the old part of the city. It was founded in 1538. Maybe six, seven thousand students here now."

---

[2] The oldest *continuous* university in the hemisphere is the University of San Marcas in Peru, founded in 1551. The Autonomous University of Santo Domingo was out of operation for several years.

Above and below: Communist signs deck buildings on the University campus in Santo Domingo. *At right:* A few signs still remain from the revolution, but the author found the Dominican people "friendly."

On the steps of the Architecture building of the University, the author was accused of being a CIA agent. He and his accuser debated the revolutionary work of Christ before a large crowd of students. (See p. 175.)

Suddenly I spotted the Communist hammer and sickle on one of the banners. Howard realized my shock and said, "This is the hotbed of agitation. By tradition the campus is off limits to police. They aren't nearly all Communists, probably just a small percentage. But the Communists make a lot of noise and put up their banners. A few days ago they illegally flew the Communist flag above the Dominican flag for a short while."

"Any evangelical missionaries working with the students?"

Howard frowned. "None that I've heard of. I wish we had someone down here. I wish I could myself, but I'm not that type. See that hill overlooking the campus? Every time I pass here, I dream of a center up there to reach these students. It's really a shame we aren't doing anything here. Here is where the trouble starts. Here is where the future leaders of the country are trained. Here is where minds are open to the gospel. It's a shame and a pity that we evangelicals aren't smarter than we are."

He was getting wound up again. "No mission can succeed without national leadership. On this campus is the raw material. But they've got to be won first. They're not going to be won the way we're going at it."

A knot of students realized we had slowed down and curiously glanced our way. Howard waved at them and smiled. "If they look at me, I wave," he said. "If they're hitchhiking, I pick them up. Sure, they're impatient and want today's problems solved yesterday. But if you're down here long enough, you'll see why they feel this way. They're ready to grasp at any straw."

Five minutes later we were back at the house. An elderly Dominican couple, the Fabio Herreras, were waiting. We exchanged pleasantries and Howard said aside, "They are good friends and have been a great help to us. Don Fabio was secretary of state to the president when Reid Cabral was in office. I could call him day or night."

Howard clicked on the ham set. "The band isn't big

enough for us all to talk at once," he said. "So one guy volunteers to be the net control for the Western Hemisphere. Right now that's Phil—K4CRU in Miami.

"HI8XHS," he said and I heard a voice answer back, "Good morning, Howard. How are things in Santo Domingo?"

"Fine and dandy, Phil. I need to talk to Julian in Chicago."

"Roger Dodger," the net control said. "I'll round him up for you."

Julian's voice from Chicago came crackling through the receiver. It was a bit distorted. The men exchanged call letters, and Howard said, "Let's go down five kilocycles and see if there's a hole in the rocks."

He spun the dial and called again. Julian came in more clearly. "I'm reading you loud and clear, Howard. Over."

"Charlie Brown and Roger Dodger. I need to make a phone patch to a Sister down in Homewood. Can you help me? Over."

"I've always got time to help you, Howard. Give me the phone number."

I stood behind Howard and listened until the telephone connection was made. Then I slipped across the street to change to a suit and tie and get some recording tape and film while Howard was doing the patch. When I returned the Herreras were gone and an American had arrived.

He was Bud Dodson, a mild-mannered, dark-haired youth, in his twenties, I guessed; he spoke with an Ozark farm boy twang. He had come to the D.R. via the Peace Corps "to do something on my own, to see a new culture and people." He had stayed on with AID to assist Dominican self-help groups in special projects. "This may be a community school, social center, or medical clinic," he explained. "We try to get the little guy involved in helping his own community."

"Yes," he said in reply to my question, "I was here during the revolution. I helped Howard by seeing he got the food and medicine for the areas he worked. No one shot at me, but I could hear the bullets whizzing about. How would I describe his work?"—and he looked at Howard—"fantastic, I guess. He has so many friends. No one feels he's obligated to anybody except to God.

"Take the rehabilitation center for crippled children here in Santo Domingo, now the only one of its kind in the country. Howard should take you there. He found out they needed desperately some equipment—wheelchairs, braces, and such. He told AID about it and we made a grant of $5,000. Then Howard got on the radio and called his doctor friends. They bought the stuff in the States at a good price and shipped it here. That's what I mean. When he comes to us about something we know he has no self-interest. The Dominicans know that, too."

The AID man mentioned he knew other missionaries—"all good people, but Howard is the real go-getter. He gets into social programs, health programs—you name it, he's in it if it's for the good of people. To tell the truth, I don't really see how he has time for converting and building churches. He stays too busy helping people."

The AID man and Howard discussed another medical project which both felt was needed. Just as he was leaving, Dorothy Dell came in with an apple pie. "Could you run this down to Don Pedro's?" she asked Howard.

Howard took the pie and we got into the car.

He stopped a few minutes later before a beautiful Spanish colonial home nestled under giant coconut palms. A chubby, white-haired, well-dressed Dominican man greeted Howard with an *abrazo*.[3] Howard introduced him as Don Pedro Purcell, the Dominican ambassador for American affairs responsible for all the Dominican embassies and consulates in the Americas. He handed him the pie and said, "A little gift. I hope you enjoy it."

Don Pedro invited us into his den, where he had a ham

---

[3] Latin hug used by good friends when they meet.

set like Howard's. I saw on the wall the framed constitution of the radio club to which both men belonged.
Howard Shoemake's signature was attached to it with
several Dominican names.

Howard placed his hand on Don Pedro's shoulder and
looked at me. "My license expired six months before the
revolution. At that time the U.S. Federal Communications Commission was refusing to give ham licenses to
resident Dominicans in the United States. The Dominican
Government, knowing this, was not required to recipro-
cate and give licenses to Americans down here. Don Pedro
stood behind me and made himself personally responsible
for anything I said or did with the radio. He's a good
friend."

On our way to another appointment, Howard talked
about friendship. "Most of my Dominican friends are not
evangelicals. Many probably will never join my church.
But they are still good, loyal friends. To me a friend is not
somebody who always agrees with me, nor someone who
doesn't see my faults. He is someone who defends me at
my back and is loyal when I need him."

Howard slowed the Rambler at an intersection, then
pulled over and stopped. A slight, dark-skinned man was
waving to him. "I'll only be a minute," he said and got
out. When he got back he explained that the man was a
doctor friend who needed some medicine. "Catholic or
evangelical?" I asked.

"I haven't got to know him well enough to ask," he
replied. "Down here I go slow about digging into a man's
personal beliefs. I prefer that he bring them out without
my asking. But we're friends and both interested in the
medical problems of this country."

I remembered what Bud Dodson, the AID man, had
said: "I don't see how he has time for converting and
building churches." I was beginning to feel the same way.
I wondered: Was Howard Shoemake really doing the
work of a Baptist missionary?

"I scratch my head and wonder, 'Why did God open that door?' The only answer that comes is that I am God's servant." H.S.

5

THE ROD OF GOD

Calle Conde is to downtown Santo Domingo what State Street is to Chicago or Fifth Avenue to New York. Smart stores display the latest mini-fashions from Paris and New York.

The shopping area of Calle Conde is relatively new, having been rebuilt since the hurricane of 1930. That hurricane, the most disastrous to hit the Americas in the twentieth century, left two thousand dead and only six hundred buildings standing in the capital. Strangely, it was the Spanish colonial buildings in the old city that withstood the storm. These are on and near the last four blocks of Calle Conde, which ends at the docks.

Here is a history buff's paradise. The Cathedral of Santa Maria, America's first, faces Columbus Park, which borders on Calle Conde. Begun in 1514 and completed in

1540, the cathedral encases the majestic marble tomb of
Columbus, priceless jewels, and treasures including the
crown of Queen Isabella. Or so I heard and read. The
gates remained chained shut during my entire stay in
Santo Domingo.

So did the Alcazar, the Hilton of the Conquistadors,
built by Don Diego Colon, son of Columbus. What hostel
wouldn't be proud to list the famous "guests" who
stopped at the Alcazar: Ponce de Leon, founder of San
Juan and discoverer of Florida; Francisco Pizarro,
nemesis of the Inca kings of Peru; Hernan Cortes, conqueror of Mexico's Aztecs; Nunez Balboa, discoverer of
the Pacific; and Alonso de Ojeda, conqueror of Venezuela.
They all slept and feasted here.

Nearby is the Casa del Cordon, or House of the Cord,
so named because of the monk's girdle carved in stone
high above the doorway. Columbus' son lived here before
the Alcazar was completed. Here, also, the English pirate,
Francis Drake, exacted a king's ransom of jewels and gold
from Santo Domingo when he seized the city in 1586.

I was disappointed at not getting to explore these
historical treasures. A walk around showed one reason
why they were closed. Those colorful exports of affluent
North America, tourists, were not to be seen. The tourist
trade was so bad that a pimp and his prostitute pursued
me for three blocks before giving up.

"It's too bad," Howard said, referring not to the pimp's
failure but to the absence of tourists. "The country needs
the tourist dollars. Apparently, they're scared somebody
will shoot them. There's really no reason for this fear.
Haven't you noticed how friendly everyone is?"

(Subsequently I discovered another reason for the poor
tourist trade when I visited the Government Tourism
Office. The employees moved around as if they were four
hundred years old. They had not one photograph of historical sites for the press. Compared to its Mexican
counterpart which I had visited in Mexico City three

Columbus is said to have tied his ship to a tree whose stump (right) is still standing in Santo Domingo's harbor.

The Alcazar (below) which Columbus built between 1514 and 1540 was the "Hilton" of the conquistadores. Ponce de Leon, Pizarro, Cortes, Balboa, and the pirate Sir Francis Drake all stayed here.

months before, the Dominican operation seemed to border on the ridiculous.)

I did notice how friendly the Dominicans were, especially when I was with Howard Shoemake. Looking like Wilt Chamberlain at a Boy Scout picnic (only a slight exaggeration!), Howard's towering form could easily be seen in the downtown crowds. Everywhere he was accosted by Dominicans who greeted him with smiles, pats on the back, and handshakes or *abrazos* depending upon how well they knew him. He took time to stop and chat and ask about families while I stood by impatiently.

"You don't rush up to a Dominican friend and say hello and good-by," he lectured me. "You take time to talk. No one down here is in too much of a hurry for friendship." Remembering the tourist office, I muttered under my impatient breath, "No one is in a hurry down here for anything."

Later I gasped, "Where did you get to know all these people?" when we finally got into the car after the first exhausting afternoon downtown.

"The school, the radio club, civil defense, doctors' meetings, and a lot of other places," he replied. "I didn't meet most of them in church, that's for sure."

"Good thing you're a missionary," I said. "You'd never make it as a pastor back in the States. You wouldn't even be considered a good layman in some churches."

"You're probably right," Howard replied. "Since my last furlough I've decided neither a pastor nor a layman can be both a good Baptist and a community-minded person in many of our churches."

Later I talked to a U.S. diplomat about the friendliness of the Dominicans. He said, "It's different between us and Shoemake. I doubt if the Dominicans really think of him as a foreigner, despite his physical size. He's so much involved in their affairs and speaks Spanish so well that they think of him as one of their own. With those of us who represent the U.S. Government, it's different. Most

Dominicans are friendly, but we do have to be careful where we go. The Embassy has often asked us not to go downtown after dark and not to drive or ride at night in cars with diplomatic license plates."

My image of Shoemake as a Christian humanitarian was solidifying. Yet all I had heard from him and others who knew him suggested that he had changed radically since coming to the Dominican Republic. One morning while Howard was taking the boys to school, I asked Dorothy Dell if she had seen a change.

"He has acquired some different interests," she said, "but he is still the same person. He has always been intense about whatever happens to be his current interest. In Texas and in Colombia and Ecuador, he lived and breathed church building. Sometimes he worked sixteen hours a day supervising volunteer workers at construction sites. His hobby then was photography. We've got hundreds of pictures which you can dig through when you have time. But he doesn't care much about cameras now. During the revolution he didn't take a single picture."

"What's he most interested in now?"

She laughed and pointed to the ham set. "That. Medicine. Civil defense. The school. And community problems. The little church he pastors, of course." She paused. "Maybe I'm giving you the wrong impression. He's interested in those things because they relate to people. Maybe that's the difference in him now. He has a much stronger interest now in people and their immediate needs."

"But what happened to change him?"

Dorothy Dell is not a talkative person. Quiet, unassuming, she usually speaks the least in a group. This time she seemed hesitant to reply. Finally she said, "He had a very personal spiritual experience between the time he returned from his survey and the time he brought the family down to live. Get him to tell you about it."

Howard returned in a few minutes, and we talked.

"I've always thought I was following God's guidance," he confided. "But as I told you, I mistook activity for spirituality. There were times when Dorothy Dell and I felt closer to God. One was when Jimmy fell from a balcony in Ecuador and broke his neck. It was a miracle we got him on a plane after they told us no seats were available. It was another miracle that he survived and is now in good health. I think we felt closer to God then because we had come to the end of our resources and had to let God undertake.

"But when we were preparing to come as a family to the D.R., something different happened. The door that seemed to be open so wide when I made the survey appeared to be closing. We made a trip to New Orleans from Fort Worth to get our entry papers at the Dominican Consulate. The man in the office was new, and he couldn't find the documents the director of immigration in Santo Domingo had promised me he would send. We went on to a missionary orientation conference in North Carolina and swung back by New Orleans.

"The morning after we got back to New Orleans, I awoke about 4:30 and began reading the Bible. Some verses in Isaiah stood out like neon lights. The message was addressed to Cyrus, but that morning at least God was giving them to me. Several phrases lodged in my mind. '. . . I will loose the loins of kings . . . and the gates shall not be shut; I will go before thee, and make the crooked places straight: I will break in pieces the gates of brass, and cut in sunder the bars of iron: And I will give thee the treasures of darkness, and hidden riches of secret places, that thou mayest know that I, the Lord, which call thee by thy name, am the God of Israel.'[1] It was as if God were saying, 'Howard Shoemake, I will let you witness to presidents and cabinet ministers if you will let me direct your steps.'

"We had come into the hotel dead tired, and I had

---

[1] Isaiah 45:1-3.

promised Dorothy Dell I would let her sleep late and go to the beauty parlor. But after I read this, I got so excited I grabbed her and said, 'Woman, wake up." She turned over and mumbled something about it being still dark outside. But I got her up and read her the passage. She didn't get too excited, but merely said in her sweet way, 'However the Lord leads you, I'm with you.'

"After awhile we ate breakfast, and I left her at the beauty parlor and went on to the Dominican consulate. The consul saw me coming and began shaking his head. I walked up to him, gave him the date and the name of the man who fixed my papers in Santo Domingo. I begged him to look some more. He shrugged and halfheartedly started going through stacks of envelopes. Well, he found my stuff in the last bunch of envelopes in the last drawer of his desk.

"He did some fancy apologizing and fixed up our papers. I scooted over to the beauty shop and told Dorothy Dell that everything was all clear. We drove back to Fort Worth and started packing. While there, a now dear friend named L. S. Rowland called and invited Dorothy Dell and me to eat with him. I had married him and his wife twenty years before. He said I hadn't charged him anything for the wedding and he had always been grateful. We took him up on the invitation and enjoyed good fellowship. He asked us to name some of the things we needed in beginning a new work. We did, and he said he wanted to do something for us.

"Several weeks passed; with only four or five days left, we hadn't heard from him. Suddenly he called and said he'd like to give me a ham radio set and for me to pick one out in an electronics store. That really bowled me over. I had not thought much about a radio and didn't know what I would do if I had one. I thought there were a lot of things we needed worse.

"I asked a friend from our Radio and Television Commission to go with me. We settled on a rig that cost about a thousand dollars. Right then I didn't know one end of an antenna from the other.

"We packed the radio and went to Galveston, Texas, where we took a ship to Santo Domingo. Everything cleared customs but the radio. The customs men sent me to see the director of communications, he apologized for the delay and began dictating a letter to release the radio. While his secretary was typing the letter, he said, 'Why don't you make application for your station license now?' He handed me a form and helped me fill it out. I explained that I didn't know how to operate the radio. He said not to worry, that I could learn. About three weeks later, I got my license and have been operating ever since. The director of communications, incidentally, was Thomas Cortinas, whom you met in Miami."

Howard leaned back and looked at the ham equipment that extended across one end of the room. "That radio was the rod of God that rolled back the waters before me and opened countless doors of opportunity to serve."

"Give me examples," I asked.

"Well, a few weeks after Cortinas sent my license, I was invited to join a club of Dominican hams. Hams hadn't been too plentiful during Trujillo's time. There were only about twenty-five when he was killed; there are three hundred now. I got in just when the club was building up. They asked me to help write the constitution which you saw at Don Pedro's house. Some of the hams had children in the Carol Morgan School. They encouraged me to run for the school board. I did and was elected to alternate membership.

"A few months later, the Dominicans formed a civil defense committee to help out during hurricanes and other natural disasters. Because I happened to be the only Protestant some of them knew, they asked me to represent Protestants on the committee. I knew it would take a lot of time, but I felt my job was to serve the country."

Howard stopped and looked embarrassed. "If you print

some of this stuff, people will think I'm bragging. I don't mean to. I just happened to be available."

"Friend," I said, "I'm here to get this story. I intend to talk to a lot of other people, but I'd rather get it from the horse's mouth first."

I pointed to the stack of round film cans and square tape cans that filled two bookshelves. "Radio and TV programs?"

"Yes," he said, "and this is another ministry related to the ham radio. A few weeks after I joined the club, a club member and I were talking about religious programs. He asked me what Baptists were doing and I told him about our series of 'This Is the Answer' dramas in Spanish. This man was Waldo Pons, the chief engineer for the Government television and radio network. He asked if I could get an audition film for them. Fortunately, I had brought one with me from the Radio and Television Commission in Fort Worth.

"They auditioned the film and decided to test it on Sunday night on prime time without previous announcement. To my knowledge, this was the first time they had telecast a religious program. When the program ended their switchboard lit up like a Christmas tree. They couldn't handle all the calls. This was on Sunday night when evangelicals were in church services.

"Waldo came back to our house and asked, 'When can you get the whole series?' I said, 'Maybe in a couple of months. I'll write Fort Worth.' He said, 'That isn't quick enough. Have it sent air express; we'll pay the charges.'

"We got the initial series of Spanish dramas from Fort Worth and everything else the Radio and TV Commission had available in Spanish for radio and television. Besides the telecasts, about twenty radio stations have since used our programs, and stations in other countries picked up the telecast on recommendation from the Dominicans."

"How much did this cost the Foreign Mission Board?" I asked.

"Not a *centavo* for air time."

"Are the programs still on?"

"Some of the radio programs are still running. But I picked up the television films a few days ago. They had been rerun to death on half a dozen different time periods. The Radio and TV Commission is putting together a new series now."

Howard grinned. "I forgot to tell you something. When I first came here I bought some time on one radio station for the Baptist hour in Spanish. This didn't work out. The station didn't run it at the same time each week. Nobody knew when it was coming on. I haven't tried to buy any time since."

"How about the listener response?"

"I'm glad you asked that. We've had letters from all over the country. Our Box 880 is the best-known address in the country. You can read some of the letters at the church office. Over two hundred have taken our Bible correspondence course. Wherever we've gone to start new churches, we've found doors open because of the programs."

Later that Friday evening, Howard and I drove to his downtown church. At nine o'clock the street in front of the ancient three-story green frame building was dotted with Dominican boys. They were darting back and forth across the street and into the shadows of laurel, mahogany, and rubber trees that clustered in a small park facing the ocean. When Howard stopped a dozen ran to the car window, shouting "Meester Shoemake! How are you?" Howard talked to them for a few minutes.

"Some nights I come down alone and talk to them about their problems" he confided as we walked toward the church. "Only one is not friendly. His father is a local Communist. When trouble starts everybody blames the kids. They have nothing to do, no place to play but the streets. I can't feel hard toward them."

Howard had already told me the history of the building

and how he had managed to rent the first floor. During Trujillo times, the building had housed the socially prominent Union Club with a bar and casino on the floor. A year and a half after arriving in the D.R., Howard had seen a newspaper ad offering the first floor for rent. He contacted the club's director, who asked what he would use the space for. Howard frankly admitted he wanted to start a Baptist church and "anything else we want to develop there." The man, a personal friend of Pope Paul and president of the Catholic Dominican Youth organization, tried to avoid renting the space. Howard insisted his offer be submitted to the club's board of directors. They voted unanimously to rent the space for $250 a month. Some of them knew Howard from radio club, civil defense, and Carol Morgan School functions.

Why had he waited eighteen months to begin Baptist services?

"Dorothy Dell and I knew that as Baptists we wanted to count our chickens and see immediate results. Yet we felt we should wait and pray. More than once Dorothy Dell wondered what we could say in our letters home. She was afraid our friends at home would think I had gone off the deep end in community activities."

Howard stopped on the sidewalk and pointed toward the second floor. The walls were peppered with bullet holes. "A company of rebels was up there during the revolution. They never bothered our floor." He turned and pointed across Ozama Bay, into which Columbus had sailed. "U.S. troops and Dominican Government soldiers were on that strip of peninsula. Later they occupied the park and forced the rebels out from upstairs."

We walked inside. I saw where a bullet had lodged just above the pulpit. "I keep the bullet on my desk at home as a souvenir," Howard said.

The largest room had been converted into a sanctuary and furnished with pews and pulpit furniture. Sunday School and Training Union record boards hung on either side of the pulpit, which stood where the bar had been. Forty-two had been in Sunday School the previous Sunday. Howard chuckled. "Small potatoes compared to churches back home; but we try to make a little go a long way."

A game room for Ping-Pong and a youth Sunday School class was adjacent to the sanctuary. Gambling tables once had stood here. A smaller room in the back held supplies of medicine. I glanced at the assortment of drugs. "Why so much streptomycin?"

"We got lots of infections and fevers," Howard replied. "MAP now has a warehouse near our house. I keep a few things here to pick up when I'm visiting in the neighborhood."

He fondled a bottle of pills. "This medicine got us three doctors for the Lord and influenced another," he said. "Two of them are turning out to be full-time medical missionaries. You'll meet them later."

One of the church's nineteen members was in the church office answering radio and television mail. "We paid someone to do it," Howard noted, "until Dona Ana volunteered."

Howard introduced me to Ana de Pena, a buxom graying woman with a soft voice. Her family, she said, had a farm in the country which her husband worked weekdays. She had moved into the city to be with her four children who attended the university. She saw the church sign, began coming, and was converted. Answering broadcast mail was the least she could do for the Lord. She couldn't think of taking pay, she said.

"Our membership isn't large by U.S. standards," Howard said. "But we have seven university graduates."

We walked to the door. "This is part of the old city. At one time it was considered quite aristocratic. But in recent years many homes have been divided into apartments and rented out. Some of our members will soon be moving to the suburbs west of here. We'll probably lose them to a

Howard Shoemake is the pastor of the Baptist Temple in the old section of Santo Domingo. The building (below) used to house the Union Club in Trujillo's time. The congregation rents the first floor.

Top: Dona Ana, a member of the Baptist Temple, answers mail received in response to television and radio programs. *Bottom:* Pro-communist newspaper mural decorates a wall near the church.

church our newest missionary is starting out there. This is really a hard neighborhood in which to start a Baptist church, but I felt we should begin in the inner city. (Several evangelical missionaries volunteered the same opinion to me in later interviews. One said, "Howard started a church where nobody else would.")

He looked at his watch. "In a couple of minutes a lady is coming to see me about a personal problem. Maybe you'd like to walk around the neighborhood. It's safe," he added.

"I'll go check the post office for a letter from my wife," I said, "if you'll give me directions."

"You can't miss it," he said and proceeded to outline my route.

As I walked along the sidewalk beside the church, I noticed a newspaper mural on the wall. It was a collection of newspaper headlines and pictures cleverly prepared to arouse animosity against the U.S. and Dominican governments. One picture showed U.S. soldiers thrusting bayonets at Viet Cong prisoners lying helpless on the ground. Another article showed pictures of Marx and Lenin above a favorable article on Communist social progress. Another showed headlines from a Dominican newspaper: MORE CHILDREN DIE OF GASTROENTERITIS.

(Later I saw similar anti-U.S. propaganda on the walls of the Baptist church in Santiago. I asked Howard why they did not get rid of the propaganda, and he shrugged. "What would be the use? They'd put it right back up.")

I turned the corner and walked up a narrow street toward Calle Conde. The narrow two- and three-story houses were built wall to wall, with open doors and windows to catch any breeze. They were plastered and painted in garish pastels: blue, pink, yellow, green. Some were still scarred by bullets from the revolution. Political slogans—*Viva Bosch, Viva Socialista, Viva Cuba,* with an occasional "Go Home, Yankee" were scattered along the walls. (Howard told me later not to be concerned about the few "Go Home, Yankee" signs I saw. "They're an embarrassment to almost all Dominicans," he said.)

The streets swarmed with cars and carts and children selling fish they had caught in the bay. Lottery vendors, carrying wooden frames with tickets strung on wire, pestered me on every corner. A teenage girl wearing bright yellow slacks swayed on the sidewalk with a transistor at her ear. Through an open doorway I saw a circle of pre-school children swaying to a Latin rhythm band. A record blared, "Pancho, the Great Revolutionary," to the tune of "Davy Crockett." The mythical "Pancho" had spoken English at two, shot two men at three, gone to jail at five, fallen in love at six, married at seven, and was killed for becoming a revoluntionary at nine. He was, the song said, "brave like a lion; small, but a killer."

A few houses farther on, the solemn-faced Che Guevera in guerilla garb peered at me from a newspaper poster under the scrawled caption: *Viva Los Guerillos.* Farther along, I passed a line of dark-eyed men slumped against the wall, eying me suspiciously. "Don't worry when people stare at you," Howard said another day. "That's *libertad."*

I reached the post office, which sits only a stone's throw from the giant stump of the ceiba tree where Columbus is supposed to have tied his ships. Box 880 had a letter for me plus a handful of letters and cards addressed to the radio and television programs. I looked at the barely legible handwriting on one. One of three and a half million Dominicans, I thought. One who deserves to know the truth that can set men free.

"People must participate in the solutions to their own problems. We can kill their self-respect and self-identity by making them dependent upon us." H.S.

6

THE LEGACY OF TRUJILLO

The warm November days passed swiftly. I talked with dozens of people—Dominicans and resident Americans—in Santo Domingo and made four trips into the country. I met the Shoemakes' denominational colleagues: three young couples, all first termers, all eager and enthusiastic in evangelism and church building. More about them later.

I would sooner go on a bear hunt without a rifle than research a book without a tape recorder. But with most Dominicans I had to take fast notes, then later put these notes on tape. In my several years of free lancing I have never met people so apprehensive of a recorder. Some answered my questions only when assured by Howard that I was "nonpolitical."

After reading the history of the D.R. and especially the

terror tactics of Trujillo, I came to understand their re-
luctance to talk. It is generally admitted that Trujillo
still has a host of friends underground, in the country and
abroad. The monument at the spot of his assassination
has been knocked down and a warning scrawled, "THIS
IS WHAT WILL HAPPEN TO COMMUNISTS."

The sadistic and clever Trujillo used every conceivable
terror device to maintain his rule. He made the D.R. one
vast concentration camp. Every few miles on each highway Trujillo's soldiers maintained a checkpoint—two
bumps in the road with a sentry post between them.
Every driver stopped, showed his identification card number, destination, and intended time of return. Drivers
could be searched and often were.

No one could ever be sure he was safe. Telephones were
tapped, hotel rooms bugged, mail opened. Informers could
be a man's brother, wife, or lifelong friends. Everyone
whispered, feared, mistrusted, and squirmed when soldiers
approached.

One afternoon I talked with one of the thousands of
Trujillo victims. I promised not to use the name of the
young husband who faced me. His thin hands twitched
nervously as he recalled his first taste of terror. A few
days after an ill-fated attempt to overthrow the dictator
—June 14, 1959 [1]—he, then only fourteen, and some
young teens were talking on the street about the incident.

"Suddenly the police descended on us," he said. "They
beat me up, broke my lower jaw in fourteen places and
my arm in three places, and threw me in prison. I was

---

[1] On this date Dominican exiles, backed by Venezuelan President Betancourt
and Cuban Premier Castro (his Communist ideology was not yet known),
landed in the D.R. by boat and plane in an attempt to overthrow Trujillo. The
dictator's soldiers captured the invaders and later had them tortured to death.
Shortly afterward, three young sisters of the prominent Mirabal family, who had
been active in the anti-Trujillo student underground, were murdered. From
these tragedies sprang the June 14th political party which had a fairly large following for several years, but is now generally acknowledged to be controlled by
the extreme left.

later released, then imprisoned again after the dictator's assassination by Ramifis Trujillo, the son. Many of my friends were killed by the Trujillos," he said. "My uncle was beaten into insanity. It was hard then and now for young people to be lighthearted in this country."

Another afternoon a pretty young Dominican girl, barely twenty-one, obviously embarrassed, stared at the floor as she recalled to me Trujillo's method of satisfying his legendary sexual appetite.

"Each week his procurers selected a group of girls for his bed. Persuasion was used on girls and their families who resisted. One of my girl friends said no. Her father lost his job. Then the police came and took her clothes. I knew about other cases where the girls and their families disappeared."

One evening Howard and I went to a high Dominican official's house. He talked quite freely until I mentioned the name Trujillo. Instantly his face froze into a mask. Though we talked awhile longer, the interview for all practical reasons ended then. Later Howard said, "He worked in Trujillo's government and is afraid of losing his job. Actually every man of ability in the country worked for Trujillo. They had no other choice. Many, like the man we talked with tonight, still serve in the government. Some are corrupt, but not all. I don't buy this guilt-by-association idea."

My sources, both written and oral, gave Trujillo credit for efficiency, technical progress, and peace keeping. The "Benefactor of the Fatherland" (one of the many titles he bestowed on himself) jailed Communists, built roads, sanitation and water-supply systems, irrigation systems, luxury hotels, a jet airport, hospitals, housing projects, schools, and many industries. He jerked the country out of the quicksand of bankruptcy and established financial stability—but all for a cruel price. The money came from high taxes, higher prices, and "contributions."

The benefits went mainly to the Trujillos, who finally

Visiting dignitaries under the Trujillo regime saw only the show places of modernized Santo Domingo, as George Washington Avenue (bottom) with its replica of the Washington Monument, and the huge globe in

front of the "Fair Grounds" where Trujillo built a display of government buildings. They did not see the poverty, the disease and starvation that existed, and still exist—and that Howard Shoemake and others are working to combat.

owned a large portion of almost every industry except drugs (for example, twelve out of sixteen sugar mills, and employed 80 percent of the nation's workers.) Trujillo catered to his own vanity by building dozens of private mansions where servants stood ready to pamper and please him at a moment's notice. His wardrobe held more than ten thousand neckties (his particular mania), two thousand suits and uniforms, and five hundred pairs of shoes.

His vanity seemed to know no limits. He decreed the "era of Trujillo"—reminiscent of the Roman Caesars. He erected thousands of monuments to himself and once was heard to wail his regrets that he governed so small a country. He enforced the national slogan "God and Trujillo," and would have had it "Trujillo and God" except for the opposition of the Catholic Church. Cardinal Spellman did please him immensely by publicly embracing him on a visit and calling him "benefactor of the Church." Cordell Hull, the U.S. Secretary of State under President Roosevelt, acclaimed him to be "a splendid President . . . outstanding among all those in the American nations." Trujillo reciprocated by naming broad avenues after both men, the names of which were quickly changed after his death.

Of course poverty, illiteracy, and disease flourished under Trujillo. But the outside world did not know about these until after his death. Visiting statesmen and journalists saw only what he wished them to see.

Terrorism and corruption increased during the last five years of his rule. A motley band of twenty Dominicans who shared a common revulsion for the dictator began plotting his death. They watched and waited for an opportunity to strike.

About 9:30 P.M., May 30, 1961, Trujillo and his chauffeur left Santo Domingo for one of his palaces in San Cristobal. Two carloads of gunmen fell in behind. A third car blocked the highway about two miles up the black seacoast. As the dictator's car slowed for the road-block, one car sped alongside. A shotgun blast tore through the side window and into Trujillo's side. The bleeding despot ordered his chauffeur to stop and fight. The assassins blasted him to the ground; then one jumped on his face and shouted, "This ——— will kill no more people."

Trujillo's family and hard-core supporters instituted a reign of terror. They had hundreds arrested and tortured. Eighteen of the twenty plotters died before the Trujillo machine was dismantled.

Eighteen months after the assassination Dr. Juan Bosch was freely elected. He took office on February 27, 1963. (The Shoemakes had arrived the previous July.) A new constitution was proclaimed on April 29.

Four months later the Bosch government fell to a military coup. It was a dramatic day for Howard Shoe-make; an opportunity to act in a time of great need. The date was September 6, 1963, a day when what happened in Santo Domingo sent shock waves around the world. The great experiment in democracy seemed to have failed.

A 5:30 A.M. the Shoemakes heard poundings on their door. Howard switched on the outside lights and peeked through a side window to see policemen standing with machine guns.

He opened the door and greeted them. *"Buenos dias, senores.* What's the trouble?"

A man whom Howard knew stepped forward and spoke, "President Bosch's government has fallen. He surrendered to the generals at the palace about an hour ago. We are under orders to pick up all ham radios for security reasons. We came here first because we know you have all the names and addresses."

Howard called the man aside. "All this will do is cause some bitter enemies. Give us a little time and we will ask the hams to go off the air voluntarily. They will do it."

"Who will you call first?"

"Don Pedro Purcell, the president of our ham club. You know him. He is Ambassador for American affairs in the Dominican foreign office."

At the mention of Pedro Purcell's name, the officer stepped back. "OK, call him. We'll wait."

Howard called his friend and explained the situation. "The police are here now," Howard said, "and will be at your house in a few minutes. I think they will let the radios stay if we can persuade the hams to stay off the air."

"All right," Don Pedro replied. "I'll help you."

In less than half an hour, every ham had been notified and the police were satisfied.

An hour later Howard got a call from civil defense authorities to come to headquarters for a meeting. "Hurricane Edith is headed straight for us and may be here tonight," a Red Cross official said. "We need to get our communication system working."

Howard raised his hand. "How can we when the police have put us off the air?"

A representative of the police called out, "Who are the hams that have been working with civil defense?"

Someone read off a list of names which included Howard and Bob Meyers, a Baptist Mid-Missions missionary.

The police officer took down the names and said, "We'll try to get clearance for these to go back on the air."

Howard returned home to watch television. The Government station was broadcasting live from the palace. He listened to the military leaders give their reasons for the coup. President Bosch was leading the nation into economic chaos, they charged. He had permitted Communists to move into positions of power.

President Kennedy had supported the Bosch regime. He immediately ordered diplomatic relations suspended and the U.S. ambassador and AID mission home.

An uneasy calm settled over the city as refugees sought shelter in foreign embassies. Armed soldiers patrolled the downtown area. Rain fell in sheets, perhaps discouraging angry crowds from forming.

Howard got into his car and began driving around. The car had a receiver but no transmitter. He listened. About 1:00 P.M. he heard a voice on the radio. "Howard, if you are listening, go to the police station. They have something for you."

He drove to the police station and was met at the door by a man with some papers. "Here are permits for five of you to go back on the air and help civil defense with the hurricane." Howard looked at the permits. One was for himself, one for Bob Meyers. He breathed a prayer of thanks.

He returned home and turned on the radio. A weather station in Puerto Rico reported the winds were a hundred miles an hour at the center and it extended for sixty miles. Edith was small but dangerous.

Early in the evening he drove to Red Cross headquarters and found men milling around debating what to do. The Bosch government had fallen under military pressure; now no one seemed to know who was in command of the new government.

That night the hurricane shifted and began moving east on a course slightly south of Santo Domingo and toward the D.R.'s Samana Peninsula, which juts into the Caribbean toward South America.

Howard remained at Red Cross headquarters all night, while in other parts of the city diplomats worked feverishly to defuse the time bomb of discontent that was sputtering among political leaders.

On Friday the winds and rains rolled over Santo Domingo. Reports of flooding came from Barahona on the coast of the Samana Peninsula. "We're going out in a plane to warn the people," someone told Howard. "Come with us."

Howard shook his head. "The political situation is too bad for a foreigner to get involved."

Later another plane prepared to leave. "You belong with us," a Dominican said. "We do not think of you as a foreigner."

He climbed into the plane with a newsman and three officials. They reached the danger area in about forty-five minutes and began flying a basket-weave pattern at three hundred to one thousand feet, watching for stranded people and warning residents to flee.

Howard stayed on duty through Friday night. By Saturday morning the storm danger had passed and the floods were receding. Farm crops in the peninsula area had been heavily damaged, but not one life had been lost.

A ruling *Triumvirato* of three men assumed control of the government with the businessman Donald Reid Cabral, who was recognized as the leader of the three. It was generally accepted that they were backed by the military. The deposed President Bosch left for exile. Ambassador Martin and other top U.S. officials had already left for the States.

Howard discussed their situation with Dorothy Dell. Neither proposed leaving.

"God brought us here," he said. "He will keep us here to serve our friends."

Then he fell into bed for the first sleep he had had since Wednesday night.

Less than two months later the chilling news came that President Kennedy had been assassinated. Though diplomatic relations were suspended and Ambassador Martin was in Washington, long lines of weeping Dominicans began forming outside the U.S. embassy.

Dominican friends stopped by to see the Shoemakes and express their condolences. One seemed to speak for all. "He tried to help our country."

Howard and Dorothy Dell received the sympathies and expressed thanks. Both were very careful not to make comments on the Dominican political situation. "When we take sides," he told Dorothy Dell later, "we cut ourselves off from part of the people."

A few days later they began services in the rented Union Club building.

Eighteen tumultuous months had passed since their arrival.

"We don't have to lose our spiritual identity in order to work with someone of another faith for the good of the community. We know who we are." H.S.

7

SAVING THE BABIES

One sunny Sunday afternoon Howard and I stopped briefly at the church. I glanced at the attendance figures posted behind the pulpit. Howard saw me looking and said in his usual hoarse voice, "Sometimes I look at those figures and compare them to other churches I've pastored. I feel a little guilty, maybe because I was number conscious for so long. Why, some of my pastor friends back in Texas get that many new members in their Sunday School in one week."

He rested a huge arm on the pulpit and stared out across the vacant pews. "Maybe if I had spent more time in church development," he mused. "Maybe—but you know it's real easy to be a historian. Real easy. You can look at my work and say, 'Why didn't you do it another way?' All I can say is that I entered the door that opened, not the door that was esteemed or traditional. I served churches for twenty-three years before coming here. I've never prayed as much and tried to follow the Spirit's leadership as closely and carefully as I have here. I've never pretended to be qualified to do all that God has led me to do. But you don't stop and ask yourself, 'Am I a qualified swimmer?' when you see a child drowning. You jump in and do the best you can. That's the way it was with the rehydration program. I saw the children dying and had to jump in and do something."

I had already heard a good deal about the rehydration program. I remembered what the ex-president said in Miami, ". . . to save lives, that is the greatest benefit to my country."

Before leaving Chicago, Ray Knighton, the executive director of MAP, had given me some basic information on gastroenteritis—the major reported cause of death in the D.R. "Poor hygiene, lack of refrigeration, flies, hot weather, unclean dishes, improper food care," Knighton said, "are all factors that help bring on gastroenteritis. The actual cause in many cases," he stressed, "is infection with the dysentery bacillus or with an organism such as streptococcus.

"The symptoms are about the same regardless of the cause: sudden fever, irritability, vomiting, and diarrhea. The baby begins dehydrating, the skin turns slaty gray, the mucous membranes are parched, the temperature may rise, and stupor or convulsions may occur. In infants, death can come in twenty-four hours unless there is rehydration with suitable body fluids such as 5 percent glucose solution. Facilities and fluids for rehydration are readily available in the United States, but in the D.R. they were almost nonexistent before we started this program."

With what I already knew about gastroenteritis, I went one morning to the Dominican health ministry and talked to doctors and officials about the disease. They showed

me year-by-year mortality graphs that indicated gastroenteritis to be the number one cause of indentifiable infant
deaths. The director of health statistics said bluntly,
"Sixty percent of all deaths last year were among children
below five. At least half resulted from gastroenteritis,
maybe more, who knows. It's hard to get good reports
from the country towns."

I walked through a Santo Domingo downtown slum and
saw children playing in open sewers. At the end of an alley
stood the only water faucet for two thousand people; behind the faucet was a filthy toilet. The little girls tottered
about in filthy rags; many of the little boys were stark
naked. Their stomachs were bloated and distended, the
marks of malnutrition. They swatted feebly at the swarms
of disease-carrying flies that infested the area. Some
sucked on dirty bread that they had rescued from the
flies.

I saw a stringy-haired mother clutching an infant and
blowing on a pitifully small pile of charcoal beside the
family shack. She was more fortunate than other mothers
who could not afford the price of charcoal to boil water, a
most necessary precaution in any part of Santo Domingo.

An hour of such sightseeing was all I could stomach. I
knew that many of these children would never live to be
school-age; those fortunate (or unfortunate) enough to
survive would be retarded. Was it enough for a missionary
to come in and quote Bible verses and teach the children
choruses that "go over" with happy well-fed children who
romp on green lawns in America? What could one do here
in the name of Christ?

In eight years as a pastor and six as a journalist, I have
seen a good share of human misery. But never had I seen
anything like this. I walked away in a daze, thinking of
what I had seen and what Howard had told me earlier:
"If your children were starving to death or dying in filth,
you'd do anything—even steal or riot. These poor people
are not Communists. They don't know what communism

is. All they know is they're sick and hungry."

The chain of events that led to Howard's medical work began during the summer of 1964 in Dallas. A physician who was a deacon at the First Baptist Church and member of the Christian Medical Society learned that his fellow deacon Fred Lange would be making a business trip to the Dominican Republic. "Look into the medical problems and see if there is some way CMS can help," he asked Lange.

Fred Lange talked to Dominican health officials, who told him about the severity of gastroenteritis among Dominican children. He also met Howard Shoemake and was impressed by the missionary's desire to help the country.

Back in Dallas, Lange reported his findings and impressions to his doctor friend. The doctor passed the information on to Ray Knighton, then the executive director of the Christian Medical Society.

Knighton asked Dr. C. Everett Koop of Philadelphia and Henry Harvey, associate director for CMS's overseas Medical Assistance Programs (MAP)[1] to accompany him to the D.R. in November, 1964, for a survey. Howard Shoemake met them at the Santo Domingo airport and after briefing them took them to the Dominican health ministry. There the minister of health and several Dominican doctors joined the survey team. They traveled for a week. They visited cities and villages, looked at medical facilities, gathered statistics, and stopped frequently at lower-class homes to observe how mothers were rearing their children. Again and again, Dr. Koop pointed to stricken babies and said, "That little one will be dead within forty-eight hours if something isn't done."

They quickly came to some shocking conclusions: (1) Mothers were ignorant of health procedures in childbirth and child care. Government health education was both

---

[1] In 1965 MAP and CMS became separate organizations, with Knighton becoming executive director of MAP.

inadequate and incomprehensible to the mothers. (2) Impure water and lack of sanitation made it easy for children, especially babies, to become infected with gastroenteritis. (3) Most doctors were in the large cities, and most of these had neither sufficient knowledge nor medical equipment to treat gastroenteritis. (4) There were only about eighty registered nurses in the whole country; hospital patient care was largely in the hands of inadequately trained practical nurses. (5) Only one hospital, the Reid Cabral Children's Hospital in Santo Domingo, had facilities and fluids to rehydrate babies in danger of dying from dehydration.

The American and Dominican doctors estimated gastroenteritis was killing thirteen thousand children a year. All agreed the biggest need was public health education. "Everything else is a stop-gap," Dr. Koop said.

In Santiago the doctors helped set up a unique nursing school. The Free Methodist mission provided two missionary nurse instructors. Two local doctors volunteered to teach part time. The Catholic University furnished buildings and laboratories. Local hospitals welcomed the student nurses for on-the-job training.

The minister of health pledged to revise the public health education manuals and make them easier to understand. But there remained the urgent need to save the thousands of children who would surely die before preventive programs could take effect. There were no medical missionaries serving in the country. The Dominican Evangelical Church had closed the only mission hospital in 1959. They did not know a single Dominican Protestant doctor.

CMS, the doctors informed Howard and the minister of health, was not a mission board and could not send permanent medical missionaries. CMS could send short-term help and through its MAP affiliate provide fluids and scalp-vein kits for intravenous insertion of the fluids into dehydrating babies. The short-term doctors and medical students could train Dominican doctors to use the kits. Rehydration units with beds and a supply of scalp-vein kits and fluids could be set up within hospitals and clinics throughout the country.

The health minister beamed at these proposals. "Wonderful. Let's talk to the President and get his approval."

Donald Reid Cabral was then the recognized head of the triumvirate appointed to serve after the bloodless overthrow of President Bosch. He received the survey team with enthusiasm. After the minister of health explained the program, he smiled and said, "My government welcomes your help and will cooperate to the fullest with your director down here. We will excuse the duty on all the medicine and equipment you wish to bring in.

Afterward, Howard asked Ray Knighton who the director would be.

"You," Knighton said.

"Whoa," Howard replied quickly. "I can't do this and my other work, too. I'm already in civil defense and was just elected president of the school board for The Carol Morgan School. We're trying to upgrade the school and get money for a new building. I'm helping the Santo Domingo Chamber of Commerce, AID, and the Ford Foundation set up a business school for office workers.[2] I have a church and am expected to be a missionary for my denomination. A new Baptist missionary couple, Bill and Ann Coffman, have arrived and started work across the Ozama River. I need to spend time with them."

"We'll pay you a salary, of course," Knighton went on. "What can be more important than saving the lives of babies?"

"The salary doesn't matter. We are well provided for by our mission board."

---

[2] This school now has about four hundred students training to be secretaries, clerks, office managers, etc. Howard translated for Dr. Hamden Forkner, whom the Ford Foundation sent to help the Chamber of Commerce. He also helped plan the budget and prepare a list of equipment needed for the school.

"Then you can hire a secretary, and we'll pay her salary and all other expenses that go with the project."

Howard talked to Dorothy Dell. "How can you do it?" she asked. "You'll have to neglect some other work."

"What is my work?" he asked aloud. "It's helping people."

The telephone rang. It was a missionary parent protesting against increased school expenses. "We must have quality education for our children," Howard told him. "Better curriculum and equipment and higher teacher salaries are essential."

"But this will mean higher tuition which some of us can't afford," the caller sputtered.

Howard knew the man had a point. Unlike the Shoemakes, his support came directly from churches and individuals who might balk at contributing more money for tuition. The Southern Baptist Foreign Mission Board would pay the increased tuition for the Shoemake children. Tuition for children of U.S. Government workers and businessmen would also be included in expense allowances.

"We're going to oppose you on this, Howard," the missionary continued. "I'm warning you now."

Howard grimaced as he hung up the phone. "The school must be upgraded," he told Dorothy Dell.

A few days later Howard talked again with U.S. AID officials about the school. They were happy about the Dominican Government's gift of land for a new school and would ask Washington for a building construction grant. "A good school will keep quality people on our staff down here," one told Howard. "We're behind your upgrading program 100 percent."

Howard's decision to become involved with the CMS/ MAP program was not easy. He finally concluded, as he told Dorothy Dell, that "this was a door of service the Lord had opened and I must enter."

He utilized one of the rented rooms in the Union Club

building for medicine storage and set up the MAP office in their home. Betty Lister, who lived next door and spoke English, became the MAP secretary. Julian Cannon, a blind ham operator in Chicago, gladly agreed to set up phone patches for Howard with Ray Knighton in suburban Wheaton.

The first crates of fluids, scalp-vein kits, beds, and other necessary rehydration equipment arrived at the Santo Domingo docks in January. Howard speeded the shipment through customs within an amazing twenty-four hours. A team of nine Christian doctors and four medical students, recruited for short-term service, followed the medicine.

Howard, the minister of health, and the CMS team moved rapidly to get the first center ready for dedication in the Moscoso Puello Hospital in Santo Domingo. Beds were set up. Quantities of dextrose and glucose fluids were brought in.

The program for this first dedication set the pattern for the rest: a luncheon; recognition of special guests; a devotion by a visiting Christian doctor; a short address by a government official; and a prayer of dedication.

President Donald Reid Cabral came to speak at the first dedication. When Howard arrived with a doctor, the seats at the head table with the President were filled. They sat down near the back wall. An official saw Howard and escorted him to a seat beside the President.

The ceremonies were televised and reported in detail by the newspapers. The only irritant to Howard was the rum served at the luncheons. He drank Cokes and made no objections. After the second center was dedicated, the minister of health called to say, "We've decided not to serve alcohol at future dedications. It doesn't mix well with your prayers."

The rehydration centers were set up in every population center of the country. After each dedication the MAP medical team stayed for a few days to train personnel before moving to the next hospital. Within three months MAP was supplying units in twelve hospitals, and the Dominican health ministry was handling an equal number. As news spread through the countryside and city slums, hundreds of mothers began bringing their children. Some hospitals averaged forty to forty-five scalp-vein infusions each day during the peak epidemic months of January and February. Still many babies died in the arms of mothers standing in line.

When given by trained hands each infusion was amazingly simple. The baby was placed on its back and held in position by the mother. The site of injection on the scalp was cleansed with an antiseptic. The point of the needle was inserted into the vein at an oblique angle, and the force of gravity sent the life-giving fluid into the bloodstream. The rate of flow was carefully regulated, because too much too fast could balloon the infant's veins and cause them to rupture. Then the nurse or doctor placed a piece of cotton or gauze beneath the hub of the needle to hold it at an angle of about thirty degrees and anchored it in an immobile position with strips of adhesive tape. With the flow regulated, the infant could be left in the care of its mother until the infusion was completed.

As the rehydration program picked up speed and received widespread publicity, something unexpected happened. Doctors began calling Howard and identifying themselves as evangelicals. He organized about twenty into the first overseas chapter of the Christian Medical Society and began monthly meetings in his home.

The meetings took the form of a "round table" to which evangelical doctors invited their colleagues. The round table began with a short devotion, followed by a lecture and discussion on a relevant medical problem. Usually, after the round table ended in prayer several doctors remained to talk informally over coffee. One night Dr. Donald Johns, a visiting C.M.S. pediatrician from Grand

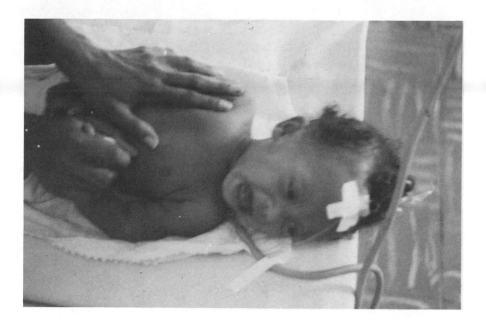

Dehydrated babies
receive life-restoring
infusions of fluids.
At right, Shoemake
and a Dominican
doctor check a baby
under treatment.

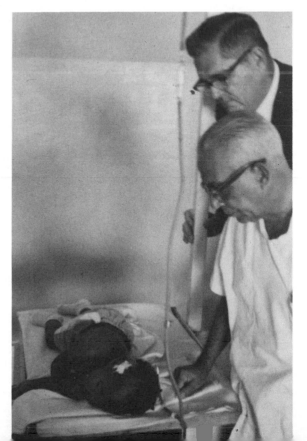

Rapids, Michigan, was the lecturer. A high Government official was present and became so interested that he stayed and talked with Dr. Johns until after midnight about spiritual matters.

Howard brought to the second round table a doctor guest who had attended a few services in his church. By birth a Catholic, Dr. Agustin Cornelio had been reading a Bible given to him by an evangelical doctor several years before. After the round table discussion Howard proposed that they close with short prayers. When the doctor next to Dr. Cornelio finished, Howard opened his mouth to pray. Suddenly Dr. Cornelio began praying.

The following week Howard ran into a Free Methodist doctor in a Santo Domingo hospital. This doctor introduced him to Dra.[3] Josefina Roman, a young gynecologist who also taught at the University of Santo Domingo Medical School. "Josefina is interested in knowing more about the Bible and how she can become a Christian," the Free Methodist doctor said. "Perhaps you can answer her questions better than I."

Howard talked with Dra. Roman for over an hour. In time, she became his second doctor convert.

He met Dra. Gladys Germosen de Mieses in a tuberculosis hospital about ten miles west of Santo Domingo. She came to the CMS doctor's round table, visited church services, and professed faith in Christ.

The fourth Dominican doctor convert was another woman, Dra. Gisela Cucurullo. Howard met Dra. Cucurullo and her husband, also a doctor, after the dedication of a rehydration center in San Juan de la Maguana. Both husband and wife had been influenced by Mennonite missionaries and had been watching "The Answer" on television. Later they moved to Santo Domingo, and the wife and daughters started attending Howard's church, where they professed faith in Christ.

Howard stayed busy with the rehydration program

---

[3] Women doctors are *"Doctora"* (Dra.) in Spanish.

during the first three months of 1965. This kept him from working in the nationwide Evangelism-in-Depth effort conducted by most evangelical churches and missionaries.

Meanwhile, the country moved steadily into a deepening crisis.

While the rehydration program was pushed, the country wilted under a disastrous drought. Only a half-inch of rain fell during the first four months of 1965. Much of the land turned to red dust. Water in Santo Domingo sometimes flowed for only two hours in the morning.

World sugar prices plummeted until it appeared the country would lose thirty million dollars in 1965 by selling sugar below production costs. Coffee and banana prices also dropped. Unemployment increased. Government workers began receiving pay in vouchers which most merchants would not accept.

Loud rumblings arose when Donald Reid Cabral, the provisional President, announced elections would not be held until September; they had been expected earlier. Rumors began spreading that once deported Communist leaders were slipping back into the country.

Ambassador W. Tapley Bennett, who had become warm friends with Howard Shoemake through Carol Morgan School activities, sent several warning messages to Washington. One in early April declared: "Little foxes, some of them red, are chewing at the grapes. It is impossible to guarantee a good harvest in view of many unfavorable aspects of local scene. It is, however, fair to say that a dimunition of our effort or failure to act will result in bitter wine."

Powerful military leaders began plotting. Some wanted Bosch, who had been overthrown eighteen months before, returned to power. Others wanted to replace Reid Cabral with a junta that would restore special privileges he had taken from them. Communist agitators saw the deepening divisions as an opportunity for their own profit. The preceding November a secret meeting of Latin American

Communist parties had been held in Havana. In January Russia's TASS released a statement of the conference that reaffirmed the "duty" of Communists everywhere to support "the national liberation struggle," including the struggle in the Dominican Republic. From this time the foreign Communist (especially Cuban) propaganda attacks against the Reid Cabral regime became increasingly provocative. Analysts predicted an explosion was forthcoming.

The last of twelve MAP rehydration centers was dedicated in early April, 1965. One morning Howard, Mr. and Mrs. Ray Knighton, Dr. and Mrs. Martin Andrews, and Fred Lange (who had come for the last dedication) called at the palace and found the hallways full of armed guards. At Howard's request and with President Reid Cabral's consent, Martin Andrews led in prayer for the country and for the success of the rehydration centers.

Later Howard returned to the palace for a short conference. A short, dark-haired sergeant accosted him at the steps.

"Mr. Shoemake, forgive me for taking your time. My name is Ramon Vargas. I've heard that you have many doctor friends in the United States. My little daughter has a very bad heart. No doctor can help her here. Will you help her get an operation in your country?"

Howard looked into the man's pleading dark eyes. He could not find it in his heart to say no. "A doctor is here now from Oklahoma City," he told the guard. "You get the medical report and X-rays on your daughter and call me."

The guard took Howard's telephone number and gripped his hand. "I will get the report," he said huskily. "Thank you. Thank you."

After examining the Dominican doctor's report and X-rays, Dr. Andrews told Howard, "The main problem seems to be that too much blood is being pushed through the lungs and not enough through her body. It might be

Left: Dr. Martin Andrews of Oklahoma City and Howard Shoemake inspect some newly arrived medicines.

Below: medical supplies are trucked from the Santo Domingo docks to the MAP warehouse which is now near the Shoemake home.

Shortly before the 1965 revolution, Howard Shoemake and U.S. visitors met with President Reid Cabral (in the white suit above). From Cabral, to the right are J. Raymond Knighton, Mrs. Knighton (face out of picture), Mrs. Martin Andrews, Dr. Martin Andrews, Shoemake, the Secretary of Health, and Fred Lange who helped initiate MAP medical work in the D. R. A presidential aide leans over Shoemake's shoulder. *Below:* On March 29, 1968, the Dominican government awarded J. Raymond Knighton the country's second highest honor—knighthood in the Order of Christopher Columbus. Lic. Pablo Jaime Vinas, Sub-Secretary of Foreign Affairs, made the presentation, while Howard Shoemake and Dr. Ralph Blocksma of Grand Rapids, Michigan, looked on.

correctable. But the girl might also die during the operation."

Howard went back to the palace and gave this information to the father. "Even if we can get her to the United States," he warned, "the operation might fail."

Sergeant Vargas wiped his eyes. "If she doesn't go, she will die anyway. What do we have to lose?"

"OK," Howard said. "We'll see what can be done."

The Andrews' took the diagnostic material and flew home to Oklahoma City. There Dr. Andrews talked to Dr. Allen Greer, a heart surgeon, about the case. Dr. Greer offered his services free if the girl could be brought to Oklahoma City.

Dr. Andrews radioed Howard through ham operator Travis Harris to tell him of the surgeon's offer. He stated also that the Free Methodist Deaconness Hospital in Oklahoma City would donate all in-patient services.

Howard notified the father and they began making plans. But before little Ingrid could be put on a plane, the country exploded in civil war.

"I've never felt the urge to stay home as much as I did during my last furlough. I asked a preacher friend what he would do if riots came in his community. He didn't know. I said, 'If you don't know now, you won't know then.'" H.S.

8

THE FIRE AND THE FURY

The fuse on the time bomb of political unrest was burning faster when Howard Shoemake and the MAP team visited provisional President Reid Cabral in the palace. The country seethed with rumors of revolution.

Observers in world capitals eyed the tiny country with increased concern. Following Trujillo's assassination, the first experiment in democracy had failed. Would the country have another chance at free elections? Would it have a Castro type of revolution? Would another rightist dictator seize power and tyrannize the Dominicans into submission?

The political pundits speculated while most Dominican evangelicals promoted their first nationwide Evangelism-in-Depth crusade and Howard Shoemake kept the MAP rehydration centers running smoothly.

President Reid Cabral was caught between the pinchers of right and left. His popularity sagged. Reports flew through Santo Domingo that several military men were angry because he had cut off their sources of graft.

The provisional leader sensed that a coup was coming. He expected it to take place at the February 27 [1] Army Training School just west of Santo Domingo on the Santiago highway. He later stated: "Since I didn't want bloodshed, I went there on April 19 with Army Chief of Staff General Marcos Rivera Cuesta and my military aide on the pretense of inspecting the school. This would give them a chance to take me prisoner, and bloodshed would be avoided. But they didn't do anything."

Five days later, General Rivera Cuesta returned to the February 27 encampment to confront the suspected plotters. The conspirators took him prisoner, then went to his headquarters, ransacked his desk, and found the names of other officers who were suspect by the Government. They alerted these officers, called a radio station, and declared to the world that the revolt had begun, the twenty-fourth since the nation won independence in 1841.

Saturday, April 24, 1965, became a date the Shoemake family will never forget.

The Dominican revolution was front-page news in the U.S. for weeks to come. Millions of Americans watched it nightly over drinks and potato chips. Numerous magazine articles and several books debated the judgment of the United States in intervening.

Even if I were qualified, I would not give an opinion in this book on the rightness or wrongness of U.S. intervention. To do so might impede the nonpolitical service of Howard Shoemake.

Dozens of people in the D.R. told me that Howard enjoyed the friendship and support of many Dominicans because they knew he was not partisan in politics. A sign, "DON'T TALK POLITICS, IT'S TOO NICE A DAY,"

---

[1] Named for the date Dominicans celebrate as their Independence Day.

hung above his ham radio set during the civil war.

Howard still refuses to "talk politics" about the revolution except to say, "There was probably right and wrong on both sides." This simple judgment is enough (and in agreement with many analysts) for him to keep friendships on all sides.

All with whom I talked in Santo Domingo praised his work during the revolution. Not a few called him "next to the U.S. Ambassador in influence." One high-ranking U.S. diplomat who must go unnamed said he had "more influence" with the Dominicans than did the ambassador.

All but two of the hundreds of U.S. writers in Santo Domingo missed him during the civil war. The late Jules Dubois, Latin-American representative for the *Chicago Tribune,* came to the Shoemake house several times to use the ham radio. Apparently, he never saw a story in Howard. Kenneth Gilmore, the distinguished *Reader's Digest* writer, sought him as a source for his article on "The Truth About Santo Domingo," May, 1966; but at Howard's request he did not directly quote him.

Howard kept no diary and took no pictures during the tragic days. He can be an entertaining story-teller when in the mood. However, his memory is notoriously poor about details of events.

By adding Howard's modest remembrances to the accounts of those who were intimately involved with his activities during the revolution, I pieced together the following account. Because the first few days were so confusing[2] and eventful, I put the remainder of this chapter in time sequence.

---

[2] Better analysts than I have tried to understand and keep track of the political intrigues in the D.R. Once in exasperation, former U.S. Ambassador John Bartlow Martin called the country a "lunatic asylum." Hopefully, readers will understand my predicament in trying to be nonpolitical and make sense of the chaos that characterized the first few weeks of the Dominican civil war. There were, by actual count, twenty-six political parties active in the country before the revolution.

Friday, April 23

U.S. Ambassador W. Tapley Bennett, Jr., left to visit his gravely ill mother in Georgia. He had talked to her the preceding day by radio phone patch from the Shoemake home.

Howard and Jimmy Shoemake, then an eighth grader, worked in the MAP medicine storeroom at the church, preparing shipments of bottled glucose and dextrose for the rehydration centers. They returned before dark to their rented house on Abraham Lincoln Avenue in the western part of the capital.

Saturday, April 24

Howard went in the morning to the Pan American office on Calle Conde to make final arrangements for flying the Vargas girl and her parents to Oklahoma City for her heart surgery.

His two sons, Jimmy and Ricky, walked to a store near *Parque Indepencia* (Independence Park) on an errand. They saw crowds shouting in the park, *"Viva Bosch! Libertad!"* and taxi drivers circling the park with horns blowing. When they reported this to Howard, he said, "Something's really up. We'd better scoot home fast."

At home they learned that a rebel group had announced their revolt over the radio. The family clustered around the radio and television sets for more news. Radio Santo Domingo, the main Government station, was denying the revolt. Suddenly they heard the noise of scuffling. Another voice broke in and shouted, "Reid Cabral's government has fallen! Go into the streets, Dominicans, and celebrate! Viva Bosch!" They heard more scuffling, then the first announcer's voice again: "The government has not fallen. President Reid Cabral is still in office."

The President heard the confusing broadcasts and hurried to the palace. Aides told him his opponents had control of only two battalions of soldiers. He alerted Santo Domingo police and several army units. He ordered the tank commanders to attack the rebels. But the generals who had once pledged loyalty to him sat on their hands.

By midafternoon the rebels were broadcasting on four radio stations. They called themselves "Constitutionalists" and demanded the restoration of Bosch and constitutional government.

Charge d'Affaires William B. Connett reported to Washington that Reid Cabral's government was in trouble but had not been overthrown. The U.S. embassy had received reports that Communist elements were organizing with speed, though apparently they had been caught unaware by the timing of the rebellion. President Johnson sent the aircraft carrier *Boxer*, with fifteen hundred marines aboard, and other naval craft into Dominican waters.

American citizens began arriving and asking Howard to make phone patches. He took each in turn, warning, "Don't breathe a word about politics." When the phone patches were made, Howard calmed the two maids, Gisela and Maria (both of whom had become Christians a few weeks before).

"The Answer" came on Santo Domingo's Government television at the usual time.

The Government station announced President Reid Cabral had decreed a curfew and had given the rebels until 5:00 A.M. to surrender or be crushed.

Sunday, April 25

The 5:00 A.M. deadline passed without action taken against the rebels. Reid Cabral had clearly lost the support of the armed forces. A thousand rebel troops moved into the capital and began distributing arms to civilians. Loyalist officers notified the U.S. embassy that they could not control the rebellion. Armed mobs began rampaging through the capital, shooting and looting. Rumors spread that Che Guevera, missing from Cuba, was in or near Santo Domingo.

Jimmy Shoemake awoke first that morning. Hearing

soldiers marching along Abraham Lincoln Avenue, he roused the others.

The soldiers passed as they ate breakfast. The family then began preparing for church. A few blocks away, Bill and Ann Coffman prepared to leave for the suburb of Ozama, on the airport side of the river, where they had started a mission church. When they learned the bridge was in the hands of rebels, they had no choice but to stay home.

An armed mob invaded the offices of the anti-Communist newspaper *Prensa Libre* and set the building afire. The director, Rafael Bonilla Aybar, took refuge in the Guatemalan embassy. Still looking for Bonilla Aybar, the mob surged up Abraham Lincoln Avenue. They found his car a few doors away from the Shoemakes' house and burned it in the street. The wide-eyed Shoemake children watched from a doorway.

Howard got a phone patch through to Dr. Frank Means, his Foreign Mission Board's secretary for Latin America. Dr. Means said, "Do as you think best, but you might want to consider getting Dorothy Dell and the children to a safer place."

At 10:30 A.M., Donald Reid Cabral resigned. A few minutes later, fifty rebel soldiers entered the palace, took him in custody, and proclaimed their allegiance to Juan Bosch.

About noon, Bosch in Puerto Rico called Rafael Molina Urena, former president of the Chamber of Deputies. He asked Molina Urena to become President pending his return.

At 3:00 P.M. the Loyalist generals at San Isidro Air Base announced they would not accept Bosch. From this point civil war became inevitable between those for and against Juan Bosch.

The Loyalists in control of the air base sent four F-51's to strafe the rebel-controlled presidential palace, about a mile from the Shoemake home. Ricky Shoemake, then eleven, was in his treehouse in a spreading almond tree. He saw the planes diving and strafing and called to the family to take cover.

The U.S. embassy refused to take sides and tried to arrange talks between the belligerents.

Fighting broke out in other parts of the city.

Pro-Bosch rebels seized families of the F-51 pilots and paraded them on television (they had taken over the Government station), threatening reprisals on them if the strafing continued.

Reid Cabral escaped from his rebel captors in the palace and fled into hiding.

Carol and Dorothy Dell sat nervously beside the television set. "The Answer" came on. "Hey, Dad," Carol squealed nervously. "The rebels are using our program, too."

Later in the evening the mob noises quieted down. The Shoemake children went to bed and slept fitfully. Howard and Dorothy Dell's bedroom window opened onto a terrace. They took turns staying awake to watch for intruders.

Monday, April 26

Santo Domingo plunged into worse chaos. The rebels (with an undetermined number of Communists mixed among them) manned radio transmitters and screamed for the "people" to take power. They broadcast stories of atrocities which they claimed were committed by their opponents. Bullets whined through the streets. Mobs attacked at will. Police were special targets. Many shed their uniforms and hid from the mobs. Youths called "Tigres" hunted the policemen. Bodies were burned in the streets and others were thrown over coral cliffs into the sea. Power, light, and water became unavailable in many parts of the city.

U.S. officials showed grave concern at repeated reports that the Communists were gaining power among the rebels.

Over three thousand U.S. citizens and nationals of other countries requested protection from the U.S. embassy. A task force of six U.S. Navy ships moved into the port of Haina, ten miles west of Santo Domingo.

Bud Gentry, the Carol Morgan School principal, brought a book of checks for Howard to sign as president of the school board. Bud gave them to the teachers before they were evacuated.

A Dominican laborer came bringing a bag of eggs "for my friend, Reverend Shoemake."

Bosch spoke on the radio from Puerto Rico; he said he could not return to the country because all Dominican airports were in the hands of his enemies.

Another film of "The Answer" came on the television set. Howard saw it and shouted, "We're on again." A man at his elbow said, "Maybe that's the only noncontroversial program they have."

Dorothy Dell helped the maids fix sandwiches for more refugees than she could count.

A missionary drove up with Dr. Merrill Tenney, dean of the Graduate School of Wheaton College. Dr. Tenney had been helping with the Evangelism-in-Depth campaign and had come from a conference of missionaries and national workers in La Vega. The revolution had stopped the evangelistic campaign in midstream. The Shoemakes invited Dr. Tenney to stay with them until he could be evacuated. "Find yourself a corner," Howard said. "You'll have plenty of company tonight."

Ricky climbed back into his treehouse to watch for planes.

Howard ignored the warning of friends and drove his new Rambler American, purchased only ten days before, to the church to get a supply of medicine. Neighborhood people greeted him joyfully. He discovered a nest of rebels encamped on the second floor. The church was unharmed, the medical supplies intact. He came away feeling that the neighborhood was in sympathy with the rebels. When he returned home, another "Answer" film was running on television.

All through the night U.S. consular officials registered Americans and Dominican nationals who wished to leave. The embassy designated the Embajador Hotel as an assembly area for the evacuees and the port of Haina as the point of departure. Evacuation was set for the next day.

Sporadic fighting continued. Howard and several men sat on the porch and watched flares light the sky. After the children were in bed, he and Dorothy Dell lay down for a short nap.

Tuesday, April 27

At 3:00 A.M. the Loyalist controlled Dominican Navy and Air Force threatened an all-out attack unless the Constitutionalist rebels agreed to a junta government. The Constitutionalists began losing heart, and their leaders started taking asylum in foreign embassies.

At 6:00 A.M. those seeking evacuation began gathering at the Hotel Embajador. A message came from the Santo Domingo chief of police and from the Constitutionalists that they could no longer assure the safety of Americans awaiting evacuation.

Howard began transporting refugees from his house to the hotel. Dr. Tenney was one. He gave Howard an autographed book about the resurrection and said if he didn't see him again on earth, he would see him in heaven.

Mobs roamed the streets. Howard feared for the safety of Dorothy Dell and the children, who had already packed their suitcases for departure.

Ambassador Bennett returned to Santo Domingo. He began immediate discussions with leaders of the warring groups.

Shortly after noon helicopters began relaying evacuees from the polo grounds in back of the Embajador Hotel to piers at Haina. Two U.S. ships, the *Ruchmakin* and *Wood County*, transferred them to the aircraft carrier *Boxer*.

Howard drove home. Dorothy Dell insisted she

People wishing to escape from the Dominican revolution were transported by helicopters from Santa Domingo to the port of Haina. *Below*, a helicopter waits to evacuate a war casualty.

wouldn't leave unless he did. "I'll take you to the helicopter and put you on," he said. She was unusually
adamant. "I won't go unless you bring your suitcase."
He finally agreed, and they began loading bags into the
car.

Meanwhile, a rebel radio announcer called for reprisals
and urged soldiers to capture the noted anti-Communist
Bonilla Aybar at the Embajador (he was not there).
Armed rebels converged on the hotel, firing wildly, ter-
rorizing the waiting evacuees, and demanding the surrender of Bonilla Aybar. It was a miracle none of the
evacuees were killed.

An Assembly of God missionary warned the Shoemakes
that a battle was going on at the hotel. Howard and
Dorothy Dell decided to wait until the smoke cleared.
She and the children went next door to a Dominican
neighbor's house.

Friends begged Howard to pull down his radio antenna.
He refused, saying, "We need it for communication."

Meetings continued between Ambassador Bennett and
the leaders of the two groups.

Men in Cuban-style uniforms appeared on rebel television, parroting Castroite slogans.

"The Answer" came on again. Someone quipped, "All
they've got is propaganda and Howard's Baptist program."

Molina Urena, who had been acting president for the
rebels, gave up and took refuge in the Colombian Embassy. Key members of his cabinet also sought asylum.
Reports poured into the U.S. embassy that Communists
were filling the vacuum in rebel leadership. Francisco
Caamano, not a Communist, took command of the Constitutionalists. He vowed to fight on.

Ambassador Bennett reported to Washington that he
was trying to get a cease-fire and promote talks between
the two sides. He stated his belief that Communists were
moving to take control of the rebels.

The evacuation proceeded in an orderly manner at the hotel after the rebels, who had shot over the heads of the evacuees, left.

Bud Gentry rode in the helicopter with his wife, Janie, to the Haina pier and saw her on the evacuation ship. He returned to Santo Domingo to check on the Carol Morgan School. In the office with the custodian he found a soldier cradling a machine gun. Bud smiled and the soldier smiled back. He called the custodian aside and asked, "Have you had any problems?" The custodian shook his head. "Except I couldn't figure out which side the soldier was on, so I'd know how to talk."

Bud picked up a bundle of books for the Shoemake children to read and went on to Howard's house. He suggested dryly, "Let's have a school board meeting." Howard managed a grim smile.

Dusk surrendered to darkness, and an uneasy calm crept over the city. Abraham Lincoln Avenue lay quiet. The palms rustled softly above the house beside the radio aerial in the warm breeze.

No lights shone from the windows. The children, Dorothy Dell, and the maids went to bed. Howard and about twenty other refugees talked in low tones and took turns keeping watch.

Back in the United States millions of TV viewers got the latest news on the crisis. Commentators speculated that Washington would act soon.

Wednesday, April 28

Santo Domingo moved toward complete anarchy. Mobs continued to roam the streets, burning and looting.

Loyalist generals declared the formation of a military junta with Colonel Pedro Bartolome Benoit of the Air Force as the dominant leader. The junta announced free elections would be forthcoming.

Leadership of the Constitutionalists rebels became more unstable and Communist-oriented, from Washington's point of view. Almost all of those who had originally revolted in support of Juan Bosch were in foreign embassies or in hiding.

Santo Domingo police officials admitted they could no longer provide protection for some three thousand Americans still in the country. Snipers began firing around the evacuation areas and around the U.S. embassy.

At 2:00 P.M. Colonel LeRoy Benoit, head of the Loyalist junta, requested twelve hundred U.S. marines be landed to restore order. Shortly after five, Ambassador Bennett cabled Washington, "American lives are in danger." A little later he asked President Johnson to "consider" intervention.

At 7:15 P.M. President Johnson and his advisers conferred with Congressional leaders. U.S. officials in Washington began calling Latin American ambassadors notifying them of U.S. action. Two and a half hours later President Johnson announced over national television that four hundred marines had landed in the Dominican Republic to "protect" the lives of Americans and other non-Dominicans.

The Shoemakes continued busy. Dorothy Dell received and supervised feeding the refugees. Carol read from the books Bud Gentry had brought. From time to time Ricky climbed into the treehouse to look for planes. Jimmy and Glenn Shoemake wondered if friends back in Texas would ever believe what was happening.

Two hospitals called Howard for medicine. They were out of blood plasma and desperately needed glucose and dextrose solutions for infusions. He, Bill Coffman, and Jimmy started to the church to get a load of medicine. They had to move poles and rocks from the streets to get through. They loaded the medicines and started across the downtown area to a hospital near the Ozama River bridge. Suddenly they entered an area where planes were diving and attacking up ahead. People were running from houses and shooting at the planes with pistols. Jimmy slumped in the back seat with the medicines. Howard pulled into a side street and stopped until the planes left.

"There's another hospital closer by," he said. "We'll go there." They reached this hospital and unloaded the fluids. "Thank God!" a doctor cried when he saw the fluids. "We'll start infusions immediately."

They reached home safely. Bill left at once for his house where his wife, Ann, and their six-year-old Kay huddled in a hallway.

Darkness came. The radio brought news that the marines were landing. They turned on the television. Another "Answer" film was on TV.

The long night passed slowly.

Thursday, April 29

The Council of the Organization of American States (OAS) met in Washington but took no action on the Dominican situation.

Sporadic fighting and mob violence continued in Santo Domingo. The marine guard at the U.S. embassy came under heavy fire. Ambassador Bennett kept in constant touch with Washington. At 2:36 P.M. Bennett said direct intervention was necessary to open a safety zone for international travel.

Evacuation by helicopter continued from the Hotel Embajador. The OAS Council convened again at 10:00 P.M. and finally passed a resolution calling for a cease-fire and the establishment of an international safety zone.

Throughout the day emergency calls for medicine came into the Shoemake home. Howard made a second trip to the church alone, loaded, and drove to the Reid Cabral Children's Hospital.

A doctor met him at the emergency entrance. "There are some Peace Corps volunteers here. Will you take them to their headquarters?" he asked.

Howard drove the two corpsmen to their headquarters on Independence Street. He rushed inside and found an old friend, Paul Bell, director of the Peace Corps in the Caribbean area and a former Southern Baptist missionary to Colombia.

"How did you get down here?" Bell asked.

Howard grinned. "We drove."

"We just got up from the floor," Bell said. "There's been a tank battle going on right in the front yard. Look through the window." Howard looked out and saw two disabled tanks.

Howard stayed a few moments. Then, satisfied the coast was clear, he left to get more medicine at the church.

As he drove along, he felt a sudden urge to stop and pray. He stopped at the corner where he was to turn left to go to the church and prayed, "Lord, how should I go?" A voice seemed to whisper, "Turn right."

He turned right. An instant later he heard machine-gun fire. He looked toward the street from which he had turned aside. A plane was diving and strafing right where his car would have been.

Suddenly he realized that there were no other cars moving within sight. The plane was circling to make another pass. Heart pounding, he drove slowly, keeping close to the sidewalk, until he reached a Dominican friend's house. From there he called Dorothy Dell to assure her he was safe; then he drove home without further mishap.

"Come, walk in the yard," Howard asked Dorothy Dell while the maids were preparing breakfast. "All the rioters are asleep."

They walked, talked, and prayed about evacuating. She refused to leave unless he left, too. He agreed to go with them to the ship.

They called the children, ate, put bags into the car, and drove to the Embajador. Howard asked a U.S. naval officer if he could go with his family to the ship, then return. The officer said he would have to sign himself out of the country.

Howard fidgeted, grumbled, but signed. He experienced a "sinking feeling that I was flagrantly disobeying God."

They boarded the helicopter and fifteen minutes later landed on the deck of the air craft carrier *Boxer,* which was crawling with a mass of refugees. They recognized many of their fellow missionaries. One was Ann Coffman. "That stubborn husband of mine stayed in Santo Domingo," she said.

Howard stamped his foot in disgust with himself and muttered, "I wish I was with him."

Not since 1945, when the Communists had taken over China, had Southern Baptist missionaries evacuated their posts.

"I seldom preach a sermon or even give a verse of Scripture when doing social welfare. My philosophy is that if I live what I believe, the man I serve will see it." H.S.

9

HANDS OF MERCY

The *Boxer* hovered off Dominican shores for two days and nights while taking on more refugees. The sun boiled down, burning the arms and necks of those who could not find shade. Nights were blessedly cool, and the refugees slept under blankets on the upper deck.

Back on land, Santo Domingo remained chaotic and tense. Early Friday morning, big-bellied C-130 air transports from Fort Bragg began landing and discharging the 82nd Airborne's crack fighting men. They came to help the marines open up the safety zone between the rebel Constitutionalists and the Loyalists.

The OAS finally arranged a cease-fire. The Constitutionalists, ignoring it, captured the Ozama Fortress with its enormous store of weapons. Sniper bullets thudded into the U.S. embassy.

The embassy released to the burgeoning press corps a list of fifty-eight names of Communists alleged to be helping the Constitutionalists. Some newsmen became highly critical when they discovered five of the names listed twice. On Friday evening President Johnson told the American public for the first time that "people trained outside the Dominican Republic are trying to gain control."

By Saturday morning the refugees on the *Boxer* were growing weary. Children fretted, and frayed tempers stood on edge. The helicopters kept bringing more people on board.

Suddenly the Shoemakes heard an announcement over the public address system that some refugees would be put back on land; from there they would board the LST *Wood County* at the Haina docks. When their names were called, a broad smile burst over Howard's bearish face. "I'll stay on shore," he grandly told Dorothy Dell. "That's where I'm needed."

But on shore a naval officer informed him coldly, "You'll have to go with your family."

He stamped about angrily, embarrassing Dorothy Dell. Finally he relented and consented to board the LST.

Saturday night was nightmarish on the smaller vessel. There was not enough food to go around. Rain fell in torrents. Dorothy Dell and Carol bedded down in a crowded cabin with other women and girls. Howard and his two boys struggled along the darkened deck looking for shelter. They found Paul Bell, the Peace Corps Caribbean director, and Bill Coffman also looking for a dry place to sleep. Bill, who had been one of the last to leave Santo Domingo, reported that fighting was still going on despite the OAS-proclaimed cease-fire.

They crawled into the cab of a pickup truck. A ship's officer saw them and made them move to the back. The men wiggled under a plastic cover that gave little protection from the down-pour.

Suddenly Jimmy called that he had found a tarpaulin. Howard started to get out of the pickup and caught his foot in a cord. He fell headfirst over the side of the truck, painfully bruising a shin.

The tarp was stretched over a honeycomb of reinforcement steel in which there were two-foot square openings. Here they spent the rest of the tortured night, as Howard described later, "with my feet in one hole and my posterior in another."

The LST docked at San Juan, Puerto Rico, about 1:00 P.M., Sunday. A crowd of men and boys shoved rudely ahead, preventing the women and children from going ashore first. Howard, Bill, Paul Bell, and some others stood back and waited with their families.

Late in the afternoon Howard saw a friend, Carter Ide, the director of U.S. AID in the D.R., standing on the roof over the dock. "When are you going back to Santo Domingo?" he yelled to the AID man.

"Within the hour."

"Please help me get back," Howard begged. "If I don't, I don't see how I can live with myself for leaving."

"I'll talk to Ambassador Bennett," Ide promised.

The Shoemakes did not get off the LST until after dark. They checked into the Miramar Hotel, and Howard took off the suit he had been wearing since Thursday. He gave it to the maid and said, "Throw it in the furnace. I can't stand the smell anymore."

They ordered food from room service, ate, and fell into bed.

While they slept President Johnson's special emissary, John Bartlow Martin, flew to San Juan to see Juan Bosch. Martin, a political liberal and former ambassador to the D.R., had built a close friendship with Bosch. He hoped to persuade Bosch to return to Santo Domingo—in the former ambassador's words, "to advise and assist in rebuilding the country." The United States pledged to protect Bosch from violence.

Martin held a fruitless meeting with Bosch before daybreak. Not only did Bosch refuse to return, but he insisted that the Dominican affair was a "social revolution in the typical Latin-American style."

The Shoemakes rose and had breakfast. Dorothy Dell took the children walking while Howard went to cash a check and to see if he could get a plane back to Santo Domingo.

He met a diplomat friend who told him, "Ambassador Bennett has sent a cable authorizing you to return immediately. There's a plane leaving at two o'clock. You have space on it."

Excited and elated, Howard began looking for Dorothy Dell. When he found her after two hours of searching, she said, "All of us will go back."

"No," he insisted, "you and the children can fly on to Texas. I'll send for you when it is safe."

Suddenly he remembered the check and hurried to a bank. He explained their situation; and the manager, whom he had never met before, cashed the check for several hundred dollars. Dorothy Dell, the children, Ann Coffman, and her daughter boarded a flight for Miami. Bill Coffman decided to stay in San Juan in hopes that Howard could get permission for him to return to Santo Domingo.

Howard hurried to the U.S. Government plane which had been sent to bring Juan Bosch back to Santo Domingo. He waited with the diplomatic personnel on board from 2:00 until 5:00 P.M. When Bosch still did not appear, the plane was ordered to take off.

The plane landed an hour later at the San Isidro Air Force Base. The passengers transferred to a waiting helicopter which dropped them at the Embajador. Howard went immediately to the parking lot and found his car— undamaged!

He drove to the U.S. embassy to get a pass to move in and out of the International Zone that had been opened up by U.S. troops. A crowd of about a hundred were milling around inside. Someone was trying to serve coffee from a six-cup pot.

They were talking about what President Johnson had just told the U.S. public in defending the intervention. "The situation in the Dominican Republic was one of anarchy," he had said. "There is voluminous evidence to indicate that the marines arrived just in time to avoid a major calamity. . . . The revolutionary movement took a tragic turn. Communist leaders, many of them trained in Cuba, seeing a chance to increase disorder, to gain a foothold, joined the revolution. They took increasing control. And what began as a popular democratic revolution, committed to democracy and social justice, very shortly moved and was taken over and really seized and placed into the hands of a band of Communist conspirators. Many of the original leaders of the rebellion, the followers of President Bosch, took refuge in foreign embassies because they had been superseded by other evil forces. . . . The American nations cannot, must not and will not permit the establishment of another Communist government in the Western Hemisphere."

Howard mingled with the people a few moments. After getting the pass he said abruptly, "I'm going to check on my house."

The two maids, Gisela and Maria, smiled gladly when they opened the door to his knock. The power was still off but the telephone was in order. He prayed with them and tried to calm their fears before returning to the embassy with his seventy-two-cup coffee pot. While there, he made arrangements for Bill Coffman and Bud Gentry to return from San Juan. "We need to get the school going again," he said.

An embassy officer looked at him in surprise. "Are you serious, Howard? There's no water or electricity in the city. The schoolteachers and most of the kids are gone."

Howard placed his big hand on the man's shoulder.

"This will show Dominicans that we have confidence in the country."

The American nodded. "You're right. We'll help in any way we can."

Back at the house, Howard found a 250-watt gasoline power plant in the carport. He never learned the name of the donor.

Salty Duane Luther, Texaco's manager in the D.R., came from his house across the street. He carried a can of gas. "Hi, neighbor," he said jovially. "Isn't this a hell of a revolution? Glad to see you back.'

Howard shook hands with Luther, a tall, balding man who had frankly told Howard on previous occasions that he had "no use" for missionaries. "Fugitives from labor," he had called them. Nevertheless he and Howard had become good friends.

"Fix me a martini," Luther asked.

"Lemonade is better for you," Howard replied.

Luther laughed. It was a standing joke between them. Each knew well enough where the other stood.

"Where were you when the trouble broke?" Howard asked, realizing the Luthers had not been at home before he and Dorothy Dell had left.

"Down at my beach house," Luther replied. "We couldn't get back."

"Is Marge with you?' Howard asked.

"She's in our house. Wouldn't leave the country. Said we've stuck out revolutions before in our twenty-nine years of foreign living, and she would stick this one out."

"The trouble may not be over for awhile," Howard mused.

"Probably not. We'll just have to make the best of it."

Next day refugees began pouring into Howard's house. He welcomed them, saying, "Make yourselves at home. I've got work to do."

Howard drove the white Rambler to the Red Cross headquarters that had been set up in a section of the Carol

Morgan School. Ambulances were coming and going with the dead and wounded. A crew of workers were busy doing an assortment of jobs that ranged from packaging emergency food and medicine to vaccinating hundreds to prevent an epidemic.

Franklin Polanco, a thin wiry youth, grabbed him. "Are we glad to see you!" he shouted.

Howard recognized him from civil defense work. "Who's in charge, Frank?"

Franklin pointed to himself. "Me. They didn't have much to choose from, I guess."

Howard said nothing about the absentees but asked, "How can I help?"

"Plenty," Franklin replied, "but first let me tell you our situation. All the drugstores and medicine warehouses are closed. We've got about fifty people here, including six Peace Corps fellows. We're taking the sick and wounded and medicines mainly to the Padre Billini and the Luis E. Aybar Hospital. There are three or four Peace Corps nurses at each hospital."

Howard nodded. He knew the hospitals well. Billini was in the Constitutionalist zone and Aybar north of the city. "Where are you getting medicine?"

"We're getting drugs off the *Boxer* by helicopter. Oxygen is really hard to come by. We're running out of dextrose for intravenous feeding. The hospitals have been using it in place of blood for transfusions. Don't you have some dextrose?"

"I've got some at home and at the church," Howard said. "I'll order some more from MAP."

"Can you make some deliveries down town?" Franklin asked.

"Yes, the Constitutionalists know me."

"Good. We'll be calling on you."

As Howard started to leave, Franklin called out, "Be careful," and he pointed to a chair. "A second after I got up from there, a sniper bullet plowed into it."

As Howard drove home he heard gunfire from several directions. When he arrived he hooked the radio to the power plant and called Julian in Chicago for a phone patch to Ray Knighton in nearby Wheaton. "I'm back and raring to go," he told Knighton. "But I'm running low on dextrose and medicines. You know how bad things are down here. What can you send me? Over."

Knighton's voice boomed back. "Anything we've got and I can beg from the drug companies. We'll get it over to the Glenview Naval Air Station near here and see if they won't fly it down for you."

Howard heard a truck stop outside and got up from the radio. It was loaded with packages of CARE food. "Figured you'd need it," the driver said. "Where do we stack it?"

He directed the driver to put the food in the living room. Then he called Dorothy Dell through a ham in Dallas. She, Ann Coffman, and the children had reached home safely.

He started toward the church for medicine and was stopped at a checkpoint by Constitutionalist soldiers. He explained his mission, but the soldiers refused to let him through. They called an officer, who said, "We can't let you take medicines out to aid those who are fighting against us. Not even if they are in your church."

Howard tried to explain his situation. "I'm working with the Red Cross. We want to help everyone, and must have free access in and out of all zones." He added, "If I can't take medicines out of your territory, I can't bring them in."

The rebel officer relented at this. "We will trust you. We need your help. Go get your medicines."

Howard not only got the medicines but later obtained a pass from the Constitutionalist leadership. "You're the only man beside the Papal Nuncio and the Peace Corps Director who can drive his car everywhere in the city," Franklin Polanco later told him.

On the second day after Howard returned, Francisco Caamaño, the rebel military commander, was sworn in by the Constitutionalists as their president. Caamaño disputed the charge that Communists were directing the rebels and called for withdrawal of the fourteen thousand U.S. troops on the scene.

The next day, Wednesday, May 5, the OAS assumed responsibility for supervising the cease-fire. On Thursday the OAS foreign ministers met in Washington and voted 14–5, with one abstention, to create an Inter-American Peace Force to restore peace and constitutional government in the beleaguered country.

On May 7, the Benoit junta which had been set up by the Loyalists stepped down and was replaced by a Government of National Reconstruction headed by Antonio Imbert, a military man and one of the two surviving Trujillo assassins. Imbert promptly charged the rebels with violating the OAS cease-fire and ordered his soldiers to attack a rebel pocket north of town. The Reconstruction soldiers could not attack the rebel bastion downtown (where Howard's church was located) because U.S. forces were stationed between the two Dominican forces.

Howard continued responding to calls from hospitals and shelters for medicine and food. One distress call came from a school in the northern part of the city where rebel refugees had received no new supplies for over a week. Truck drivers hauling CARE and CARITAS (Catholic Charities) were afraid to go.

Two evangelical missionaries had just arrived from Santiago and were in the house when the call came. "We'll take a load in our car," one offered.

Howard warned them the trip could be dangerous, but they insisted on going "for the experience."

A few blocks from the school they stopped at a U.S. Marine checkpoint. A sniper began firing. "Take cover," a marine ordered. They hit the dirt behind Howard's car and remained there until the sniper was silenced.

Nicaraguan troops unload supplies (above). They came to Santo Domingo under the authority of the OAS as part of the Inter-American Peace Force. *Below*, a U.S. soldier prepares to leave Santa Domingo (after a provisional government was set up) with a propaganda sign.

During the revolution U.S. Army trucks transported medicines to Howard Shoemake's house.
The supplies were donated by U.S. drug companies
through MAP—Medical Assistance Programs. *Below*, Howard makes a phone patch for three Dominican children anxious to contact their mother in
Mexico City during the revolution.

While unloading at the school, a Loyalist plane began strafing the area. "Let's get out of here," Howard shouted and ran under a porch roof.

On the way back, they stopped off at the U.S. embassy. One of the missionaries asked Howard if he had "something for a headache."

"Sure," Howard replied. "Follow me back to the house."

"No, thanks," the man said. "We're going back to Santiago. We've had all the experience we want."

On May 14 the first OAS Latin troops arrived in Santo Domingo: 250 soldiers from Honduras. More followed from other Latin countries; and on May 23 all of the foreign troops, including the U.S. soldiers, were placed under OAS authority. By the first week of June, the last U.S. marines had left, leaving behind the U.S. Airborne and Air Force units to be part of the Inter-American Peace Force. But the fighting in Santo Domingo was far from being over.

Howard had only one rule for the growing number of refugees in his house: *Don't talk politics*. When he wasn't delivering food and medicine (all stores were closed), he was at the radio set making phone patches for people who wanted to call abroad. Callers, he insisted, must not talk politics.

One morning a ranking member of the National Reconstruction Government walked up to the door and handed a letter to two soldiers who had accompanied him. "Take this back to your commander and tell him I have resigned."

Howard welcomed this refugee into the house, to join the crowd of others with varying political views. Some nights the house was so full that he slept on a cot in a walk-in closet.

Regarding United States intervention, Howard recognized that at least three attitudes prevailed among his Dominican friends: (1) bitterly opposed; (2) resigned that it was the only solution under the circumstances; (3)

relieved and grateful, but still embarrassed. He said only, "Whether right or wrong, the intervention violated the rights of the Dominicans."

He also refused to carry a weapon on his person or in the car. "I have an old dull machete around somewhere," he jokingly told Duane Luther during a particularly tense day. "It wouldn't cut crab grass."

When Luther suggested that he was foolish not to carry a gun, Howard added, "I came to save souls, not to kill people."

One happy day seven tons of MAP medicines arrived by Navy jets. At Howard's request, U.S. military trucks brought them from the San Isidro Air Base.

Later thirty-one more tons were delivered to the Shoemake residence. When it became apparent that there wasn't enough room for all the crates. Duane Luther offered his carport, garage, and dance pavilion for the balance. "This is enough to keep Santo Domingo alive for a year," he quipped.

"That may be just what we'll have to do," Howard replied.

And the fighting went on.

Ambulances shrieked along Abraham Lincoln Avenue at all hours relaying medicines from the Shoemake home to hospitals. Howard made many trips in his car at the request of the Red Cross.

One morning about ten, an emergency call came from a Dominican ham operator in the heart of the embattled Constitutionalist area. The ham's daughter, an asthmatic, had to have oxygen immediately or she would die. The ambulance drivers refused to go, saying it was too dangerous because oxygen cylinders looked like bombs. Howard said, "I'll go." Franklin Polanco took two cylinders of oxygen and slid in beside him. They made the trip and returned unharmed.

The Red Cross operated with a walkie-talkie communication system. The control unit was at Red Cross headquarters with connecting units in the Carol Morgan School, in ambulances and hospitals. When the mobile units began malfunctioning, Howard arranged for them to be flown by U.S. Air Force planes to Miami, where they were repaired by Dick Root, a ham friend who worked in the communications division of the Miami police department.

There were many casualties among noncombatants. For example, two Dominicans were crossing the golf course near the Embajador Hotel. They saw a grenade in the grass. Curious, one picked it up and pulled the pin. The explosion blew him into the air.

Robert Meyers saw the victim when he was brought in—"charred from the waist down," Meyers recalled, "the worst I'd ever seen. I started crying." Meyers had practically lived at the hospital since the outbreak of hostilities, visiting and reading the Scriptures to the wounded.

The burn victim hung onto life and remained in the hospital for several weeks. Another evangelical missionary, Leonard Beard of the West Indies Mission, helped him to trust in Christ. Later, Howard Shoemake stopped by when a doctor was preparing to do skin graft surgery. The doctor's assistant did not show up; so the doctor insisted Howard scrub and assist. He did. The patient survived and was given a $13,000 settlement by the U.S. Government because the grenade was presumed to have been dropped by a U.S. soldier.

Red Cross workers conducted periodic body hunts. They found bodies stuffed in manholes, on rooftops, in the Ozama River, and in gutters after every battle. "Just follow your nose," Franklin Polanco grimly told his ambulance drivers. One hunt accounted for 155 bodies, which the Red Cross burned in a heap to guard against disease.

On May 8 Howard went to his church in the Union Club and held the first services since the revolution had started. About a dozen worshipers sang and prayed while rebel soldiers manned positions on the second floor.

The Union Evangelical Church for English-speaking Protestants had been meeting in a school building before the revolution. Because the school was in a battle area, the church had to cease services. After Howard returned, some of the men, including U.S. Ambassador Bennett, began meeting at the home of different North Americans on Sunday afternoons for prayer and Bible study.

One afternoon Ambassador Bennett asked Howard how his ham set was doing. "I've closed it down," he said matter-of-factly.

"What's the trouble?" the ambassador inquired in concern.

"You asked me, sir, and I'll tell you," Howard said frankly. "The OAS ordered some Dominican hams to go off the air. I decided if they couldn't operate, I wouldn't."

"I'll check into that," Ambassador Bennett said and left.

Within the hour the Dominican hams were told they could go back on the air.

The doctor converts and other members of Howard's flock came to the house and helped prepare food parcels and emergency medicines for distribution to private homes. During the fighting Dr. Cornelio's wife Isabel became ill. Her blood pressure dropped rapidly and death came quietly but tragically.

Howard tried to console the slim Dominican doctor, left with three small children to raise. "Agustin, I do not understand why God permitted this to happen," Howard whispered. "I do not understand why so many people have had to die during the last weeks. But God will give strength to go on."

Dr. Cornelio brushed away the tears as he embraced Howard. "I am a new Christian," he said, "but I will not give up."

On May 10 Howard and Bud Gentry reopened the Carol Morgan School. Howard had secured permission for Bud and Bill Coffman to re-enter the country under the same umbrella as educational specialists. Bill volunteered to teach until the end of the term. The following Sunday he resumed services in Ozama.

About a half-dozen teachers and thirty students were on hand when school resumed. Most of the remaining teachers trickled back from Puerto Rico during the remainder of the week, and enrollment reached 80 by Friday—"over 100 percent increase," Bud bragged to Howard. Classes continued even when gunfire and explosions could be heard in the distance; teachers raised their voices when necessary. No other school reopened in Santo Domingo that spring.

Payrolls presented a problem because no banks were open for cashing checks. Bob Graves, a school board member and Sinclair's representative in the D.R., came to the rescue. He cashed teacher checks with money received from gasoline sales.

Later, when gasoline grew scarce Graves and Duane Luther rationed it to the most needy. Luther saw that Howard always had gasoline for his car and power plant.

It was extremely dangerous to be on the streets at night during May and early June. Howard delivered medicines only in cases of extreme emergency. "Only fools and Baptist missionaries go out at night," he told the Luthers.

Few buildings escaped the looters. Even the main post office in the rebel-controlled section was ransacked. About a week after Howard returned from San Juan, the Shoemakes' and Coffmans' mail turned up intact in the National Archives. The package included about twenty letters from viewers of "The Answer." Howard gratefully told Duane Luther, "This helps restore my faith in human nature."

Electric power remained off. Only Howard had a light plant. Neighbors joined Howard and his refugee house guests during the early evening hours. Duane Luther brought a series of "Bonanza" films which Texaco had sponsored over Santo Domingo television. The Esso man supplied "Ben Casey" dramas, and Howard added thirty-nine Baptist "Answer" dramas. They hooked up the mission's film projector and enjoyed home movies nightly for several weeks.

"The Answer" and "Bonanza" proved more popular with the Dominicans than "Ben Casey," perhaps because of Casey's surliness and cynicism. Sometimes when the sound stopped in a scene, they could hear real shooting in various parts of the city.

One night at a tense moment in "Bonanza" the projector suddenly went dead, and they heard what appeared to be gunshots behind the house. The crowd dove for the floor in anticipation of an attack. After a long, fear-filled moment, Howard suddenly realized what had happened. The power plant had run out of gas and backfired.

They also played games for amusement. During the daylight hours they enjoyed Ping-Pong and darts. One night they played "going on a trip." Howard pulled out some of his and Dorothy Dell's old clothes ("Fortunately she's in the States," he said) and passed them around. Tragedy was forgotten for a few hilarious moments as Dominicans and Americans dressed in different garbs and paraded before the group.

And there were times when they prayed and talked about eternal verities while the city and nation continued in crisis.

"I don't like to see people suffer, especially children. I have to do something about it. It's just as important to help one child as it is to preach to a multitude." H.S.

10

A NEW HEART CHAMBER FOR INGRID

Acts of heroism and compassion seldom get told during the heat of conflict. The statistics of battle, the coming and going of diplomats and mediators, political proclamations, and fighting dominate the news. This was especially true during the Dominican civil war.

There were many nonmilitary heroes in Santo Domingo during the tragic months when the city lay helpless in the grip of warfare and anarchy. Peace Corps nurses did Florence Nightingale duty in hospitals behind both rebel and Loyalist lines. They ignored jibes of "Go home, Yankee" from rebel supporters, and "Commie helpers" from a few embittered U.S. soldiers. They bound and sutured wounds by the light of candles and kerosene lamps. They helped in surgery that was done without disinfectants, anesthetics, or oxygen.

Once the Peace Corps director for the D.R. ordered the girls to leave the rebel hospitals. They begged for and obtained permission to remain. A young rebel told a Corps nurse after she had treated his wound, "You are very strange to help us so we can go out and shoot your soldiers."

Relief workers for CARE, Church World Service, and Catholic-sponsored CARITAS distributed more than ten million pounds of free food during the month of May and more in succeeding months—all paid for by the U.S. Government. Famished crowds mobbed some of the food trucks. Cries were heard, "We're not Communists. We're just hungry."

Evangelical and Catholic missionaries worked twenty-four-hour shifts in hospitals and food distribution centers. Two Catholic priests, a Cuban and a Canadian, were killed. Monsignor Emanuele Clarizo, the papal nuncio to the D.R., exposed himself to danger in frequent back-and-forth trips to the combatants' headquarters in his effort to bring peace. Only he, Howard Shoemake, and the Peace Corps director had passes to all parts of the city during the first weeks of the fighting.

Robert Meyers made hundreds of phone patches through his ham set and gave spiritual counsel to more wounded and dying than he could remember. Bill Coffman assisted with operations at Howard's house and made frequent visits to people in the vicinity of his mission church in the Ozama suburb.

But Howard Shoemake, in the words of AID's Agriculture Director Howard Harper, "was all over the city and everybody's hero. He did more things for more people than just about anybody here." Harper, who spent four years in Vietnam and three years in Iran before coming to the D.R., said, "He's the most outstanding missionary I've run across anywhere and I've run across some fine ones. He never said, 'Go do it this way, boys,' but 'Come on boys, *let's* go do it.'"

Another diplomat commented, "Howard knew the people who could help—businessmen, doctors, nuns, ham operators, diplomats, Peace Corps people, other missionaries—you name them, he knew them. And he always seemed to know who to call on in the United States for help. He made you want to help and give yourself beyond the line of duty. He not only started the ball rolling; he stayed around to keep the ball out of the gutter. No one knows how many Dominican friends he has gained by his Samaritanship."

I met one of Howard's many friends on a visit to the palace.

Built by Trujillo, the National Palace stands with massive columns and domes on a hill overlooking the sea. Howard has been there many times.

Armed guards at the gate were supposed to have searched us. (Even baseball fans are searched upon entering the stadium in Santo Domingo.) Instead they waved us through. Halfway to the twenty-eight broad stone steps Sergeant Ramon Vargas caught up with us. This was the man who in early April, 1965 (just before the revolution), had asked Howard to help his four-year-old daughter Ingrid get heart surgery in the United States. But before Ingrid and her parents could leave Santo Domingo to have the surgery done, the civil war began.

Sergeant Vargas insisted that we come to the guard station in back of the palace for refreshment. There we were literally surrounded by Dominican soldiers, who brought out chairs and served us Pepsi and candy. While we enjoyed the refreshments, Sergeant Vargas stood beside Howard's chair and told the crowd of khaki-clad men what he had done. I looked at the brown palace and thought of the contrast between the missionary and the dictator. Trujillo was known for what he had taken; Howard Shoemake for what he had given. Sergeant Vargas had been at the palace twenty-two years. He knew both men.

After awhile the Dominican sergeant turned us over to a corporal who took us into the palace for a personal tour. Except for the offices where government officials were working, he gave us a stem-to-stern tour. The great ballroom reflected the sensualities of ancient Rome. Forty-two nude female sculptures leaned off the wall near the ceiling as if they were bowing to us.

Two days later we lunched at the Vargas' small blue and yellow concrete home in the Ozama suburb. Here I learned the rest of Ingrid's story.

On the first day of the revolution Howard had visited the Pan American office on Calle Conde to make arrangements for her flight. The next day the Santo Domingo airport was closed to commercial traffic.

During the next terrible six weeks he kept working to get transportation out for Ingrid and her parents. The little girl was in imminent danger of death. Regurgitation of blood was slowly drowning her lungs. She could not swallow or breathe properly; she walked bent over and pigeon-toed. The father's friends at the palace had contributed $1,000 into a special heart fund to pay transportation costs, but this meant nothing if tickets could not be bought.

Finally Howard learned that a U.S. diplomatic plane carrying a special representative of President Johnson would be returning to Andrews Air Force Base in Washington on June 10. He set up communication with Dr. Andrews through his ham friend Travis Harris. Martin Andrews contacted Dr. Allen Greer, the heart surgeon who had recruited a team to do the surgery.

Shortly after the afternoon takeoff the air conditioning in the VIP's plane stopped working. The pilot flew the rest of the way at low altitudes to protect Ingrid's delicate lungs.

An Air Force major, a ham friend of Shoemake, met the Vargases at Andrews and took them to a hotel. Because he could not speak Spanish, he radioed Howard through the mobile unit in his car. "I have your Dominican friends in my car," he said. "Find out what they want to eat for supper and breakfast and translate back into English for me." Howard did this and then reassured the Vargas family of his prayers and that Dr. Andrews would meet them at the Oklahoma City airport. Then he called Dr. Andrews to verify the arrival in Washington.

Next morning the major put the family and Ingrid on an American Airlines Electra. The airline had on board a wheelchair and a portable oxygen unit for Ingrid. Dr. and Mrs. Andrews met them and took them to the new red brick Deaconness Hospital, where a room awaited Ingrid and an apartment in the nurses' dormitory was reserved for the parents.

An alert reporter learned about Ingrid's arrival and wrote a story. Immediately Oklahoma City newspapers, television, and radio stations began extensive coverage.

A barrage of gifts (toys, dolls, clothes) and offers to help poured into the hospital. It was as if the citizens of Oklahoma City wanted to counteract ugly world opinion that had clouded the U.S. image over the Dominican crisis. Among those who offered to help was Mrs. Paul Tuol, daughter of a Methodist missionary to Mexico, who became the interpreter.

Catheterization studies began the next day in nearby St. Anthony's Hospital. Ingrid's parents watched anxiously by closed-circuit television as Dr. William Myers, a skilled cardiologist, determined whether surgical correction of Ingrid's defect could be made. They saw the tubes being pushed through her veins upward into the heart chambers and out into the pulmonary or lung arteries. The studies showed blood pressure in Ingrid's lung arteries to be critically low. The examining cardiologists confirmed the Dominican doctor's opinions that her heart was three-chambered instead of the normal four. They realized she needed a heart wall to create a septum and prevent too much blood from flowing back into the lungs.

Two weeks later, June 26, a tracheotomy was performed. A doctor explained to her parents through Mrs. Tuol, "Persons with defects like Ingrid's sometimes have breathing difficulties following open heart surgery because of the change in blood supply to the lungs. With a tube inserted in her windpipe, we can use a respirator to help restore her normal breathing."

The hospital scheduled surgery for July 8. But Dr. Greer, the chief surgeon, became ill and had to have immediate surgery for relief of a critical intestinal obstruction. Dr. Nazih Zuhdi, a Lebanese surgeon, and Dr. John Carey, a cardiologist, offered their services; the surgery was rescheduled for July 12.

Preparations moved rapidly in an atmosphere of helpfulness. Special nurses signed up to give free round-the-clock postoperative service. St. Anthony's Hospital sent over a $125,000 cross-circulation pump. The Federal Aviation Agency sent a monitoring unit for arterial pressure from its pilot certification center in Oklahoma City. A critical need during surgery would be to maintain blood pressure within her lungs after the pressure load was shifted to her lower body.

Martin and Phillis Andrews visited and prayed with Ingrid's parents the night before the surgery. Shortly after they left at 10:30, a Spanish-speaking mystery woman slipped into the Vargas' room and warned them not to permit the operation.

About midnight a distraught nurse called the Andrews home. "Ingrid's parents are upset," she said, "and want to cancel the operation."

Dr. Andrews moaned, "Oh, no!" and called the interpreter, Mrs. Tuol. "I'll go immediately to the hospital and talk to them," she said.

Mrs. Tuol succeeded in allaying their fears. The mystery woman was never identified or heard from again.

Drs. Zudhi, Carey, Andrews, and two nurses entered the surgical suite just before noon and began last-minute preparation for the open heart surgery. Ingrid had already been carried there by her father and had been anesthetized.

Dr. Zudhi bent over the tiny form and skillfully exposed the heart. At his signal the cross-circulation pump took over pumping blood through her body.

The minutes ticked past an hour as the team worked. Dr. Zudhi sewed in a thin strip of Teflon creating the new septum. Dr. Carey applied the shocking device to re-establish the heart beat. Nothing happened. The team held their breaths while he tried again. Finally he said, "The shocker isn't working."

"There's another unit here, but it isn't sterile," one of the assisting nurses said.

Dr. Zudhi, grim-faced, said, "We'll have to chance it. We can't keep her on the pump much longer."

At first shock with this machine Ingrid's tiny heart contracted and began pulsating normally. The team sighed in collective relief.

As Dr. Zudhi prepared to sew up the incision, Drs. Carey and Andrews anxiously read the FAA's monitoring unit. Blood pressure in her lungs began dropping, evidence that the Teflon wall was holding up. But would it drop too low? A moment later they had the hoped-for answer when the lung pressure leveled off.

"The repair looks good," Dr. Zudhi told the parents through Mrs. Tuol after the operation. "Two weeks in the hospital. Then two more weeks' recuperation and she can fly back home."

The Dominican couple smiled. "We must be the happiest people anywhere," Ramon Vargas exclaimed.

That evening the parents became alarmed when Ingrid began turning blue. "She's dying," the father groaned to Mrs. Tuol. He began pacing the room and wringing his hands. The mother began to cry softly.

Mrs. Tuol tried to assure them that this was an expected after-effect from open heart surgery. But they refused to be comforted. "We should have listened to that woman who came last night," the mother shrieked. At this moment the nurse sent an urgent call for Dr. Myers, who had just come into the hospital for rounds. He quickly connected Ingrid's trachectomy to an automatic breathing machine and restored adequate oxygen exchange.

The interpreter called Dr. Andrews' home and found he had just left with his wife for a rest vacation in Colorado. Dr. Andrews' son, Mark, was there. He remembered that Howard was coming to Denton, Texas, to be with Dorothy Dell during expected surgery for a back ailment. He called Dorothy Dell's parents and found Howard had just arrived.

Mark Andrews and his married sister, Pat, met Howard at the Oklahoma City airport early the next morning. They went immediately to the hospital.

The Vargases welcomed Howard with warm *abrazos*. He read comforting passages from the Bible and tried to reassure them. He prayed and committed Ingrid into God's care.

Howard returned that afternoon to Denton to enjoy a week's rest with his family. It turned out that Dorothy Dell did not need the surgery.

An urgent call came from Santo Domingo. Could he return and help iron out some problems involved in building the new Carol Morgan High School?

Reluctantly he left Dorothy Dell and the children. "I'll get everything ready for your return," he said as he kissed her good-by. They set the date for August 27, which would allow the three younger children enough time to prepared for school in Santo Domingo.

Ingrid made slow but steady progress. The hospital took every precaution to maintain proper blood flow and oxygenation in aiding her lungs' return to normal. Finally on July 9, she was released from the hospital.

The Andrews invited the Vargas family to live a few

days in their home in case there should be unforeseen
complications. They took Ingrid riding about the city.
She marveled at the mass of automobiles and exclaimed
over and over, *"Mucho carro! Mucho carro!"*

She fell in love with the Andrews' kitten, Misty. They
romped and rolled together on the sofa in the Andrews'
family room. Gifts kept arriving until the day the Vargases boarded the plane to begin the trip home.

Ingrid treasured a zippered shirt. When visitors came
she delighted in unzipping the shirt and showing zig-zag
incision marks on her bare chest. "Zipper under the zipper," she squealed in Spanish.

On the evening before their scheduled departure, Maria
Vargas removed her amber ring and handed it to Philliss
Andrews. The doctor's wife broke into tears. "No, I can't
take it," she said trying to give it back.

"It's all I can give you," Mrs. Vargas said in broken
English. "Please take it for Ingrid."

Mrs. Andrews smiled, brushed the tears away, and
hugged her Dominican friend.

Next morning, Ingrid hugged the kitten tightly before getting into the car for the trip to the airport. When
the Andrews returned, the kitten had disappeared. They
never saw it again.

Back in Santo Domingo, the newspaper and broadcast
media had kept Dominicans informed on Ingrid's progress.
On the Friday afternoon of her arrival a camera crew
was at the airport with Howard to meet the family. A
Government helicopter was scheduled to arrive within the
hour, but Ingrid would not wait. She raced into Howard's
arms and insisted she would ride home with him.

When Howard and I lunched at the Vargas home two
years later, Ingrid appeared chipper and healthy. Wearing a narrow blue ribbon in her short black curly hair, the
six-year-old girl literally bounced across the vine-covered
porch to greet us. She leaped into Howard's arms and
hugged him tightly. "I go to school," she beamed. "I can

Ingrid Vargas (top) is a healthy, happy girl two years after her heart operation arranged for by Howard Shoemake. Here he ties her shoe on a visit to the Vargas home. Ramon Vargas, Ingrid's father, has been a member of the Palace Guards for 22 years. Howard stops to talk to the guards (bottom) when he goes to the Palace.

count and can write Papa and Mamma."

As Howard stooped to buckle the little girl's shoe, Maria Vargas came through the front door and greeted us warmly. "Ramon had to work," she said sadly. "He wanted to come so badly, but the longshoremen on strike are threatening a march to the palace."

We enjoyed a delicious Dominican national dish called *Sancocho*—a soupy mixture of chicken, yams, yucca, potatoes, cushaw, and rice—served in large bowls on a spotless white embroidered linen cloth. Peeping through the back door, I saw the outdoor charcoal fire where Mrs. Vargas had cooked the food.

Maria Vargas said that Ingrid had gone back to Oklahoma City a year after the operation for more catheterization studies; they showed her heart was in good condition. The small dark-haired mother timidly touched Howard's sleeve and added, "The doctors say she will live a normal life."

While at the Vargas home I learned the family had been attending the Ozama Baptist Church, where Bill Coffman continued to serve as pastor. Ingrid even sang a Spanish chorus for us, her curly head bobbing like a fisherman's cork on a ruffled lake as she sang.

We said good-by and walked out into the autumn heat toward the Rambler. "This is like payday for me," Howard said softly.

I looked back at little Ingrid and her mother waving from under the vines. I thought of how much time Howard must have given to this family. Suddenly he spoke, voicing my thoughts.

"The smile of that little girl is worth all the effort. No time is ever wasted serving people in Christ's name."

11

SHOEMAKES' USO

The summer of Ingrid Vargas' heart operation was hot in Santo Domingo—both in temperature and fighting. Incidents kept occurring as OAS troops (mostly from the U.S.) kept open the international corridor through the city that separated the two armies. The rebels, led by Francisco Caamaño, holed up in a two-square-mile stronghold in the old city and sniped at the intervening foreign troops. The Loyalists, led by Antonio Imbert, chafed to get across the corridor to their opponents.

On June 15 bloody fighting between OAS and rebel soldiers flared into a fury that left seventy dead and over two hundred wounded. The Padre Billini Hospital in the rebel zone was crowded with the dead and dying.

Not until mid-August—the week of the Watts riots in Los Angeles—did the Caamaño and Imbert factions agree to a provisional government set up by the OAS and headed by neutral Hector Garcia Godoy. The OAS told Garcia Godoy he could use the 10,300 OAS soldiers to police the peace. Garcia Godoy proclaimed general amnesty for both sides and begged all Dominicans to settle their differences with ballots instead of bullets. He called for the surrender of all arms. To this day no one knows how many weapons remained hidden. Some turned up over two years later in the hands of Che Guevera's rebels fighting in Bolivia.

Backed by the OAS, Garcia Godoy exiled into foreign jobs several of the most controversial leaders of both sides. Former presidents Joaquin Balaguer and Juan Bosch returned to campaign for the new elections set for June 1, 1966.

Throughout the tense summer months Howard stayed busy delivering medicine, working on school problems, visiting in the rebel-held zone around his church, supplying MAP fluids to the rehydration centers, and making phone patches. Between May 2, when he returned from Puerto Rico, and July 5, when he made a short trip to the U.S., his log showed an incredible 2,517 patches. The last was a call to world-famous heart surgeon Dr. Michael Debakey in Houston to arrange for an operation on a Dominican friend. Also during this period, a total of 406 guests had stayed one or more nights in the missionary home.

Howard made a short trip to Texas, Oklahoma, and Wheaton, Illinois in July. When he returned the provisional government had started a massive campaign to clean up the tons of garbage that had piled up in Santo Domingo. But after the garbage was hauled away, there remained the rats—thousands of the furry creatures that approached the size of rabbits, "descended from rodents Columbus brought over," people declared.

"Now I know how Pharaoh felt when the plagues descended upon him," Howard told Duane Luther as he chased a big rat with a broom. "What we need is a de-liverance."

Then he remembered a large shipment of *Triban* rat poison that had come into the MAP warehouse in Wheaton back in March. Seven train-carloads had been donated by a pharmaceutical company. Ray Knighton had mentioned it during a radio talk and wondered what MAP could do with it.

Howard quickly switched on the ham set and asked the net control to look for Julian in Chicago. A few minutes later Julian met him on a frequency and made a patch to Ray's office.

"Got any of that rat poison left?" Howard asked.

"Only two hundred tons," Ray replied. "How much do you want?"

"All of it. I'll talk to U.S. AID about paying the freight and will call you later."

Howard hurried to see his friend Howard Harper, di-rector of AID's agricultural project. "Get it," Harper said. "We'll pay the freight and get people to distribute it."

The missionary slapped the AID man on the shoulder, "We'll have a Day of the Rats."

Howard got back to Ray through Julian. The two hundred tons was loaded aboard the next ship out of Chicago bound for the D.R. The rat poison was trucked from the Santo Domingo docks to Department of Agricul-ture warehouses. Watching the unloading with Howard, a Dominican friend said, "You really are angry at the rats."

U.S. AID workers and Dominican civil servants began distributing the poison—a box at every house with in-structions to put it out on Rat Day.

Now that an uneasy peace had been established by OAS mediators, U.S. soldiers felt free to stop by the Shoemake home to use the radio for calling home and to kill time. Almost ten thousand "peace-keeping" U.S. troops still re-mained under OAS command, most of them belonging to the 82nd Airborne from Fort Bragg.

Dorothy Dell and the three younger children returned on August 27 to find the carport full of rat poison and the house full of GIs. Three lounged near the ham set waiting turns for radio calls home. Four were playing Ping-Pong. Others were watching television. A blond paratrooper sat at a table munching cookies and drinking coffee. "We like it here," he drawled when introduced. "It's like a home away from home and the U.S.O. put together."

Dorothy Dell laughed and said, "Good thing Howard warned me at the airport what to expect."

Wednesday, September 8, was scheduled as Rat Day. Unfortunately, a general strike paralyzed the city and hampered the coordinated effort. Although numbers of rats did die, the results were a disappointment to Howard and others who had worked hard to make Rat Day a success.

Chaplain Art Bell invited Howard and Bill Coffman to lead worship services for the 82nd Airborne at their encampment north of the city. Lonesome and homesick, many paratroopers opened their hearts in private counseling sessions. More than one told Howard, "Tell the Dominicans who paint those 'Yankee Go Home' signs that nobody wants us to go home worse than we do ourselves."

In November Howard, Bill, and Chaplain Bell conducted revival services at the Shoemake home for GIs and other English-speaking people. The most dramatic of several commitments came on the last night when Colonel W. H. Hard, a sandy-haired, freckled brigade commander, strode down to take Howard's hand. "I want to rededicate my life to Christ," the veteran soldier told Howard. "I hope I'm being the right example to my troops."

Howard gripped his hand and smiled back. "You are, Colonel," he whispered. "You are."

As Christmas drew near, the number of soldier visitors increased at the Shoemakes'. One very young private moved from one chair to another and exclaimed, "Look, fellows! Real chairs! Just like we have at home." He switched a lamp on. "And a real lamp that we don't have to turn off at ten o'clock."

Another visitor, ribbon-bedecked Sergeant Dooley, who had children back in North Carolina, was often parked out front when the Shoemakes returned from Sunday morning services. "Don't fix anything for me," he told Dorothy Dell. "I just came over to be with people." But Dorothy Dell always put a plate out for him.

One Sunday they found Sergeant Cooley in the house drying dishes while the maids giggled behind him. "They're laughing because Dominican men don't usually dry dishes," Howard explained.

"I enjoy it," the homesick soldier said. "I do it all the time for my wife at home."

When time came to trim the Christmas tree, plenty of uniformed helpers were on hand. After they had trimmed the tree, the GIs began parking their helmets and weapons under it as they entered the living room.

On Christmas Eve Howard and Dorothy Dell invited the troops for a songfest and cookout. Over two hundred came: Catholic and Protestant, white and Negro. Sergeant Miller, the 82nd's mess sergeant, brought a load of ground beef and grilled hamburgers in the patio throughout the afternoon. Carol singing and laughter filled the house. Late in the afternoon Ambassador and Mrs. Bennett stopped by and wished all a merry Christmas. Dominican neighbors also came to wish good cheer.

During the height of the festivities Sergeant Cooley heard Dorothy Dell exclaim, "I don't know when I'm going to get time to wrap our Christmas presents." He marched up, saluted, and said, "At your service, ma'am." He wrapped the presents.

After Christmas Howard and Dorothy Dell slipped away to observe their twenty-fifth wedding anniversary at the Luthers' beach house. Their children stayed home with the maids.

They returned for New Year's Eve services at the

church. Baptismal rites had been scheduled for the widowed Dr. Agustin Cornelio and Dra. Josefina Roman.

Dra. Germosen de Mieses met Howard at the door and said timidly, "I am ready to become an evangelical, but I do not wish to be baptized." Howard made no objection and proceeded with the baptisms. (A year later, however, Dra. Germosen de Mieses asked tearfully for baptism.)

Also in December a nun called from the Robert Reid Cabral Children's Hospital. "We sisters are grateful for the medicine you have brought our children," she said. "Will you come to the hospital for a special program for you on December 31?"

Howard promised to be at the hospital at the designated time, then forgot about it. On Monday afternoon, January 2, he was visiting around the church when a child stopped him. "Reverend Shoemake, why weren't you on television this morning when your name was called?"

He blushed in embarrassment and hurried to call the Mother Superior to apologize.

Early on January 11, a U.S. Army jeep whirled into the Shoemake driveway. A lieutenant climbed out. "We're having a parade at Camp Hutchinson this afternoon," he announced. "The colonel would like you folks to come."

Carol and Ricky overheard. "Let's go, Daddy," Carol begged. "Maybe they'll let us ride in a tank."

With the kids pulling at his sleeve, Howard accepted the invitation. They left late and reached the camp, a few miles outside the capital, with no time to spare.

Lieutenant-Colonel Gorman C. Smith grabbed Howard's hand and said, "Preacher, you come with me. Your family can sit over there with Chaplain Bell." Howard followed Colonel Smith to a stand overlooking the parade grounds.

The band struck up a stirring march and paraded by the reviewing stand. Trim lines of soldiers followed, marching in smooth cadence. Behind the soldiers came tanks.

Suddenly the marchers halted and came to attention before the reviewing stand. Colonel Smith stepped to the microphone and began reading:

"On behalf of the officers and men of the Second Battalion, 504th Infantry, I thank you for making our stay in the Dominican Republic a more pleasant and enjoyable one . . ."

Howard glanced around the stand, curious as to whom Colonel Smith was thanking.

". . . Your opening your home to us and the gracious hospitality extended to us and sponsoring our songfests and cookouts have endeared you to us in all our associations. Of special significance to us was your free giving of your time and skill as a short wave radio operator, thereby permitting us to talk to our families and loved ones in the United States."

Howard suddenly realized the colonel was talking to him. A slow grin spread over his face.

". . . The morale and high spirits of our battalion have been greatly enhanced by you and your family's generous and unselfish efforts. Though time intervene, we shall always remember the Baptist missionary family that has done so much for us in our stay in the Dominican Republic."

Colonel Smith turned and handed the letter to Howard. The band struck up again and the paraders resumed their march.

More recognition was yet to come.

One evening a Dominican who had supported the rebel Constitutionalists stopped by. "Our ham radio club [1] is having a dinner next Wednesday night. We want to invite you to be our guest of honor."

"Will it be political?" Howard asked.

The man looked pained. "Oh, no, Mr. Shoemake. If it were, we would not ask you."

---

[1] There are two ham radio clubs in Santo Domingo. Howard has friends in this club but is a member of the other.

Howard said yes, and after midweek prayer meeting at the church he drove across the city to a private home where about thirty men waited. He recognized some of them as having been very active in the rebel movement.

The leader smiled at him and said, "Our special guest is Pastor Shoemake, a true friend of all the Dominican people." The men applauded, and he continued. "We have not forgotten, Pastor, how you risked your life to bring medicine and food to our families. We are grateful and would like to give you this little certificate."

Howard stood up, took the certificate, and thanked them. "I did only what a Christian should do," he said simply. "Politics are not important when people are hungry and sick."

The men applauded again, then crowded around him for handshakes.

The mild winter gave way to a warm, wet spring. On April 24, the first anniversary of the tragic revolution, an extremist shot and killed an American civilian. Political activity intensified as political parties began campaigning for the scheduled June 1st elections. The two major candidates were the ex-presidents, Juan Bosch and Joaquin Balaguer. Howard fervently hoped that the elections would be peaceful and a stable democratic government would be established. As before, he went out of his way to display neutrality in Dominican politics.

"Some Americans may laugh and joke about the rapid changes in governments here and in other countries trying to get on their feet," he told a missionary friend. "But it isn't funny at all to those of us trying to get something done for the people. Every time the government changes, we have to make new contacts and start our programs all over again."

He was primarily concerned that the rehydration program for infants be continued. The family's upcoming furlough didn't help the situation. "This business of four years on the field and one in the States does not suit me," he told Dorothy Dell. "How can we keep the lines of communication up and be gone a year?"

"I have mixed feelings, too," she admitted. "We need the rest and the children are looking forward to going home. But what will it be like when we return?"

Howard pointed to the calendar. "We've got 3 months before time to leave. We'd better do all that we can."

So, while the Dominican politicians campaigned and some U.S. columnists speculated about the future stability of the struggling country, Howard increased his work pace and kept his fingers in half a dozen services.

One finger was in the new Carol Morgan High School which was nearing completion on the western fringe of the capital. He spent uncounted hours with school board members and personnel in upgrading the curriculum and facilities. A tuition increase was voted during a stormy open board meeting. Several missionaries opposed the increase which Howard supported with majority backing. One evening Howard spoke quietly but fervently to an opponent of the increase. "I am selfish for my children's sake," he said. "I want them to live with us and attend school."

Another busy finger was in the radio and television ministries. More stations wanted programs. More listeners wrote in for correspondence lessons. The Government television network asked for sign-on and sign-off sacred music.

And another in the many-pronged medical programs: MAP and the Christian Medical Society had become separate organizations the previous year, but Howard had continued to represent both. As director for MAP, he received and distributed fluids and other medicines to the rehydration centers. As coordinator for CMS, he continued to convene the monthly round table of doctors which met in his home. He served without salary and made reports to both organizations as well as to his own board in Richmond.

By this time he was in contact with about thirty Dominican evangelical doctors, including the new M.D. converts in his church. They wanted to participate in a service ministry that was distinctly evangelical. No evangelical medical ministry was then operating in the country, except the nurse's school which Howard had helped the Free Methodists and Catholics begin in Santiago. He proposed a downtown clinic where the CMS doctors could help needy patients. MAP, he felt, would supply the medicines.

The doctors immediately became enthusiastic about this idea. Dr. Agustin Cornelio found a location on the second floor of an ancient three-story apartment building. With the consent of MAP's U.S. office, Howard transferred a stock of medicines from the Union Club church to the new place. He and a committee of doctors agreed upon a program of operation. The clinic would be open each weekday afternoon. At least three doctors would receive patients. Each patient would be asked to pay $1.00 for the doctor's examination; the medicine needed would be free. Half of the $1.00 would go to the doctor; half to expenses. "We want people to keep their dignity," Howard stressed, "and not become totally dependent on us."

The clinic was announced in the newspapers and dedicated. Immediately swarms of poor people began flocking for treatment. They filled the small waiting room and backed up in a line that extended around the outside balcony. Drs. Gladys Germosen de Mieses, Agustin Cornelio, and Socrates Perez, a Free Methodist physician, contributed the lion's share of consulting time. At frequent intervals devotional services were held for patients waiting in line. Members from Howard's church helped in the closet-sized pharmacy and distributed tracts.

The ham radio continued to take time. He had meetings at the radio club, friendly visits from Dominican hams, and requests for phone patches to Stateside phones.

One morning Lyle Copmann, the newly appointed

director of the United States Information Agency in Santo
Domingo and a good friend, called Howard. "I've got a
request from the White House that I need your help in
fulfilling," Copmann said. He explained that a Dominican
mother from Santiago had written to President Johnson,
begging him to save her son's life. A member of the President's staff had asked Copmann to check into the request. "It's legitimate, Howard," Copmann said. "The
boy's name is Edwardo Espinal. He has a serious heart
problem that can't be corrected here."

"What can I do?" Howard asked.

"Don't you have a ham friend in Boston?"

"Jim Jacobs, KIGHT. Runs a clothing store."

"I thought you did. Call Jim and ask him to talk to Dr.
Robert E. Gross at the Children's Medical Center. I'll
send over to you some information about the boy which
you can pass along to Boston"

As soon as the information arrived, Howard asked the
net control to contact Jim Jacobs. He gave the Boston
ham the story. The boy had trouble breathing and turned
blue after periods of exertion. A Dominican doctor
thought the six-year-old boy's heart was mixing the blood
of his arteries and veins in an improper manner. The
parents were poor; the father operated a bulldozer. They
had saved $170.

Jacobs called back within the week. Dr. Gross would do
the surgery, and the hospital would provide free facilities.
Jacobs and his wife would keep the boy's mother in their
home and help them with personal expenses.

"Charlie Brown," Howard said cheerily, his usual
synonym for "Roger." "I'll get back to Lyle, and he'll arrange for visas and transportation."

Within the month the boy and his parents were flown
to Boston and successful surgery completed.

On June 1 the long-awaited elections were held as
scheduled, witnessed by forty-one observers from eighteen
Western Hemisphere countries. They reported to the OAS

their opinion that the elections were an "outstanding act of democratic purity." To the surprise of some, Joaquin Balaguer gathered 57 percent of the vote and defeated Juan Bosch. However, Bosch won a majority vote in Santo Domingo.

Bosch accepted his defeat and left for Spain, leaving Balaguer to direct the rebuilding of the country. On June 28 the Inter-American Peace Force began withdrawing, and hope for the country's democratic future seemed brighter than ever.

The Shoemakes became more and more excited as furlough time approached. They looked forward to seeing Glenn and David and other relatives at home. They anticipated the coming of two new Baptist missionary couples in the fall. With Bill and Ann Coffman already serving in the country, Howard felt the church he had started would have good guidance. The Christian doctors assured him they would carry on the downtown medical clinic. Only the future of the rehydration centers seemed in doubt, since no one but Howard was authorized to receive the MAP fluids through customs.

Dominican friends visited almost every day to say *adios*. Howard and Dorothy Dell explained the furlough system to each caller and promised to be back the following year.

On June 22 three nuns from the Robert Reid Cabral Children's Hospital came to the house. One handed Howard a small hand-carved mahogany chest, smiling timidly. "We won't tell you *adios*," she said, "but *hasta luego* [until later]. Meanwhile, we will raise our prayers to God for you and your family."

Later that week a high naval officer brought an emblem of the country. "From the Dominican Navy for your service to our country," he told Howard.

During last-minute packing a delegation of civil defense officials arrived. "You have been appointed to the National Board of Directors of Civil Defense," their spokesman said. He added, "Only six men hold this responsibility."

"But I'm a foreigner," Howard protested.

"Perhaps to some you may be a foreigner," the Dominican said. "We consider you one of us."

"Our generation is not coming up fast enough with solutions to satisfy the desperations of youth. Yes, they are often radical and want today's problems solved yesterday. There may be better ways than what they propose in some situations. But they have compassion in their hearts." H.S.

12

AND THE WORK GOES ON

Four Southern Baptist missionary couples are now in the D.R. Howard and Dorothy Dell arrived in 1962. (Howard prefers the title "pastor" in the Dominican Republic. "Missionary," he said, "is demeaning to my Dominican friends.") Bill and Ann Coffman came in 1964; Paul and Nancy Potter and Tom and Josie Ratcliffe in 1966. Bill, Tom, and Howard are Southwestern Baptist Seminary graduates. Only Paul Potter, a Missourian, is not from Texas. All four pastored several years in the U.S. before going to the D.R. None anticipated foreign mission service during college and seminary days.

The three younger couples are concentrating on church building and evangelism. They respect and admire Howard for his humanitarian efforts, but as one told me frankly, "Howard's work is not the complete mission approach, either here or anywhere else." To this Howard agreed but added, "It is the work God has led me to do in the D.R."

I visited each of the four Southern Baptist churches and two mission points in the D.R. Each situation offers challenge and potentiality for growth.

Bill Coffman, keen and dark-haired with a strong arm that has earned him the nickname "Koufax," pastors two churches. The Ozama church (across the Ozama River from the main city) had seventy-eight in Sunday School the day I was there. Bedecked with shoulder streamers, a handsome choir of sixteen Dominican youth sang with fervor and feeling; the variety of skin colors suggested what heaven will be like with all races and tongues singing God's praises.[1] When Bill extended an evangelistic invitation, four came forward, including his own eight-year-old Kay.

The Ozama church members are poor by American standards; middle-class by Dominican measures. Only one member, the treasurer, owns a car besides Bill. Most of the twenty-three members are under thirty. The church enjoys a smart new building of Dominican architecture built from a combination gift and low interest loan from Southern Baptists' annual Christmas offering for foreign missions.

"The future is bright for church building in the D.R.," Bill told me over Sunday dinner. "I have ten young men in my lay preachers' class. They take turns speaking to the church during the Thursday night midweek service. We hope to develop more training programs for future pastors, both lay and ordained."

Bill stayed in Santo Domingo during the revolution

---

[1] The Dominicans are one of the most racially mixed people on earth. A Dominican Catholic priest, Father Vasquez, wrote almost two centuries ago:
"Yesterday I was born a Spaniard.
In the afternoon I was French.
Today 'tis said I am English.
I know not what shall become of me."

(except for the week in San Juan, Puerto Rico). He made regular trips to Ozama for services and his English language class. "This class," he noted, "and my presence during the revolution helped reach the young people."

In July, 1966, the Ozama congregation began a week-day afternoon medical clinic in a wing of the church. This is staffed by Dr. Agustin Cornelio and church youth who dispense MAP medicines. "It is an effort," Bill Coffman said, "to show neighborhood people that we care."

Dr. Cornelio also serves with Dra. Gladys Germosen de Mieses at a newly opened clinic-chapel in a war-ravaged *barrio* (neighborhood) of northern Santo Domingo. Week-day patients and Sunday worshipers use the same pews in the largest room. Christian literature is available to the waiting patients, who also hear recordings of Christian radio programs in Spanish. During May, 1968, the Dominican doctors averaged seeing one hundred patients each weekday. An average of about forty attended Sunday School.

Dr. Cornelio, recently elected to be Howard's assistant pastor, preaches regularly at the new chapel.

Howard and his Dominican doctor church members started another church-related clinic this year in one of the poorest areas of the capital. Drs. Cornelio and Germosen de Mieses are now serving full time at the three self-supporting Baptist clinics. They are, in effect, full-time medical missionaries to their own people. Dra. Gisela de Cucurullo has temporarily stopped practicing in order to give full time to her teen-age daughters. Dra. Josefina Roman, the fourth Baptist doctor convert, was married recently by Howard to a New Yorker and has moved to the United States.

Bill Coffman's second church is the newly organized First Baptist Church for those who speak English.[2] There

---

[2] The Union Evangelical Church for English speakers is slightly larger in attendance (about one hundred) than the Baptist church. Most Union members are from large denominations in the U.S. which are related to the National Council of Churches.

Medical work has expanded through Howard Shoemake's encouragement. The Ozama Baptist Church operates a clinic in its church building (top and middle, opposite), and church young people help distribute drugs. A new clinic-chapel opened recently in a war-ravaged section of Santo Domingo (lower left). 1640 patients visited the clinic in its first month and around 40 attended Sunday School.

Dra. Gladys de Mieses (right) serves at this clinic and at others. So does Dr. Agustin Cornelio (bottom) standing with Dra. de Mieses and Howard Shoemake at the dedication of the new chapel. Dr. Cornelio also preaches at this chapel.

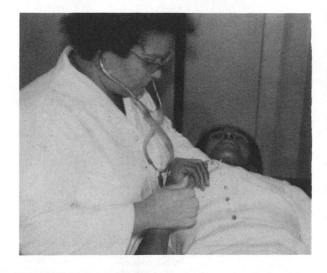

are twenty-five members and about seventy who attend regularly. This church meets spiritual needs of diplomats, U.S. AID technicians, business families, and other English-speaking residents of Santo Domingo. Arthur and Connie Trevino, second-generation Mexican-Americans, are good examples of eager workers in this church. The Trevinos both teach Sunday School, speak excellent Spanish, and assist with Baptist work in other locations. Art, a deacon, is a field agent for the Internal Revenue Bureau and on loan to the Dominican Government. Typical of other AID technicians in the church, Art said, "We have an opportunity to help this country and also serve Christ. I am one of a six-member AID team helping the Dominicans set up a training program for tax agents."

Bill and the other Southern Baptist missionaries hope that the English church can secure its own pastor from the U.S. Meanwhile, he will continue to serve as pastor until his furlough time; then Howard will assume the responsibility.

Paul and Nancy Potter live in the D.R.'s second city, historic Santiago, settled in 1500 and twice destroyed by earthquakes. Paul's congregation, meeting in a rented residence, was organized in March, 1967. With only eight baptized members, over 50 attend Sunday School. An average of 143 came daily to the first Vacation Bible School. One night 35 came to a missionary-directed training clinic for Sunday School teachers. Most of the 35 appeared to be teenagers or in their early twenties. There were more young men than young women. During the assembly between two forty-five-minute sessions, these Dominican youths sang lustily and with revolutionary fervor.

A half-dozen of the young men would like to become pastors. Typical of them is Domingo, twenty-two, who earns $5.00 a week for forty-five hours of typing and attends school in the evening. He listens to Radio Havana but does not think of Paul Potter as a "gringo." "Do-

New apartment buildings in the western part of Santo Domingo where a new church has been started.

Bill Coffman leads a Bible study for Dominican boys.

Connie Trevino teaches a Sunday school class.

mingo is more fortunate than many young men," Paul said. "He has a job and is going to school. I see men every day who have given up hope of finding employment.

"There is a great seeking and searching in this country," the fair-skinned young missionary said. "The next few years will be critical. The young people are going to attach themselves to something—to someone. If we had the personnel, we could start five new missions in Santiago within a year." (*Eds. Note: Shortly before publication, the first mission chapel of the Santiago Church opened for services.*)

Tom and Josie Ratcliffe arrived just after the Shoemakes went on their first furlough from the D.R. Neat, diplomatic, and dedicated, Tom worked for Standard Oil before going to seminary and pastored for seven years before applying for missionary appointment.

Tom pastored the congregation in downtown Santo Domingo while the Shoemakes were on furlough. "That's the hardest part of town to build a Baptist church," he admitted to me. "You can't really compare it to work in other sections of the capital. I'm glad Howard is back now."

One sunny afternoon Tom drove me through the new Mata Hambre section of western Santo Domingo where the mission had already rented a building for a new church. Pointing to a row of smart new homes, he noted, "These cost $25,000-$30,000. Only the upper middle-class can afford them, and some of them will come from the area around Howard's church. We will be the first to start a church in this neighborhood. The Pentecostals have already started home Bible classes in the neighborhood. Perhaps we will do this, too."

One Saturday the Baptists held a retreat at the West Indies Mission's assembly grounds in La Vega. One hundred and thirty-eight, mostly teenagers, came in busses and private cars for the day-long program of inspiration and recreation, over twice the number of baptized Dominicans related to S.B.C. work. Santo Domingo Baptist youth beat Santiago in softball 16-3 with missionaries serving as umpires. During rest periods boys and girls paired off to sit and talk beneath the coconut palms. There was no necking, not even hand-holding, for Dominican youth do not customarily display affection to the opposite sex in public. But it was obvious that friendships were forming and romances budding that would result in stable Christian marriages, a desperate need in the D.R.

The following Thursday I came back to La Vega for the second annual evangelical Thanksgiving retreat. Except for the Baptist Mid-Missions missionaries who were holding separate Thanksgiving services, all other evangelical missions were represented. The Free Methodists were optimistic. Dwayne Bonney, administrator of their school in Santiago, reported Free Methodist membership in the D.R. had grown from 3,150 to 3,500 during the past year. Some churches had doubled during the revolution. School enrollment in Santiago was 1350 with 80 percent of the students non-evangelicals. A goal of 10,000 members had been set to be reached by 1977.

A representative from another mission was not so optimistic. His mission had declined in both missionaries and national workers. He was critical of U.S. AID, claiming that AID had built a nun's residence.[3] He lamented that social reforms by Catholics were stealing evangelical thunder and making it harder to gain converts. He also complained about a liberal Presbyterian missionary who was promoting birth control. There seemed to be unanimous agreement among those I interviewed that Southern Baptists were the coming mission. Howard Shoemake was one reason.

"He carries a testimony into circles most of us never enter," said a seventeen-year veteran. "Those four new Baptist doctors are evidence of that. His work has ele-

---

[3] When I mentioned this criticism to an AID official in Santo Domingo, he said, "We've done some stupid things, but we're not about to do anything that foolish."

vated evangelicals in everybody's eyes. He stops the
critics who say we are outsiders who do not belong in the
Dominican culture." Other opinions of Howard's work:
"By his medical work, especially the rehydration centers,
he has demonstrated to the country that evangelicals
really care about human need." "He has put the gospel on
television and radio at no cost, something most of us never
thought possible. Everybody who has access to a television set knows who Southern Baptists are from watching 'The Answer.' "

Other reasons cited were: Southern Baptists proclaim a
positive message, not anti-Catholic but pro-gospel. ("I
don't gear my program in competition with anyone,"
Howard told me one day.) Conservative, but not
separatist. Biblical and middle-of-the-road. Evangelism
coupled with Christian training and church building. Co-
operative, but church centered.

"Some missionaries went off the deep end a few years
ago in emphasizing taboos," a veteran worker commented.
"They convinced the Dominican women in their church
that it was wrong to wear lipstick, short sleeves, and the
like. Now they'd like to change this, but can't. It's
ingrained in the tradition of their church."

A worker who is supported by "faith" contributions
from churches and individuals said bluntly, "Southern
Baptists have big money behind them. Their missionaries
get good salaries plus rent, auto, and school tuition allowances.[4] When they need to build a missionary residence
or church, money is available."

To this another independent missionary added a bit
acidly, "I'm getting sick of hearing so much brag about
Southern Baptists' big mission program. They are about

---

[4] Southern Baptist missionaries' "living support" is as follows: single missionary, $2.000; married couple, $3,600; each child under ten, $250; each child
over ten, $300. A family like the Shoemakes with four dependent children over
ten receives $4,800. Not included in this are allowances: principally rent, auto,
school tuition, partial medical expenses, and authorized transportation to and
from the field.

eleven million with about two thousand missionaries. Figure the ratio of total members to missionaries and mission giving and compare to some smaller denominations." [5]

Late one evening I tallied some figures and told Howard what he already knew. "Your Baptist colleagues are winning more people than you. What's your defense?"

He shrugged. "I guess I have none, except to say that I'm trying to follow the Lord's leadings. It just happens that He has led me in other directions, some of which may never produce any direct results for Baptists. I don't try to judge or criticize them. They are following the Lord's leadership as they see it and are doing good work. They're good preachers and evangelists and church builders."

At this time Howard had been back in the country from furlough only three and one-half months. From what I could see, he was somewhat like the Texan who strode to the airline ticket counter and asked for a ticket. When the agent asked, "Where, sir?" he replied, "Anywhere, son. I've got business all over."

Not that Howard is pompous or pushy, but he does seem to have business all over Santo Domingo. From early morning when he sips coffee with fellow hams throughout the hemisphere to late evening when he says good-night to a doctor, government official, or neighbor, he stays busy with an endless variety of people and projects. He seems to mesh the sacred with the secular until it is hard to know where either begins or ends.

Besides resuming the pastorate of the downtown church after returning from furlough, Howard renewed his deep involvement with MAP and assorted medical ministries. Upon returning from furlough, he discovered that every

[5] At the end of 1967, the Southern Baptist Foreign Mission Board reported 2,277 adult workers. These represent slightly over 11,000,000 members in 34,000 churches. The 1967 S.B.C. total budget for foreign missions was $28,022,300. This averages to $2.55 per-member annual giving with one foreign missionary for each (approx.) 5,000 members.

Howard Shoemake will go anywhere to talk to anyone—and to listen: to the Presidential Palace, to the slums, to hospitals, to homes. People know that he will listen to them. At bottom right is the priest who is working with boys from the street, Father Tomas.

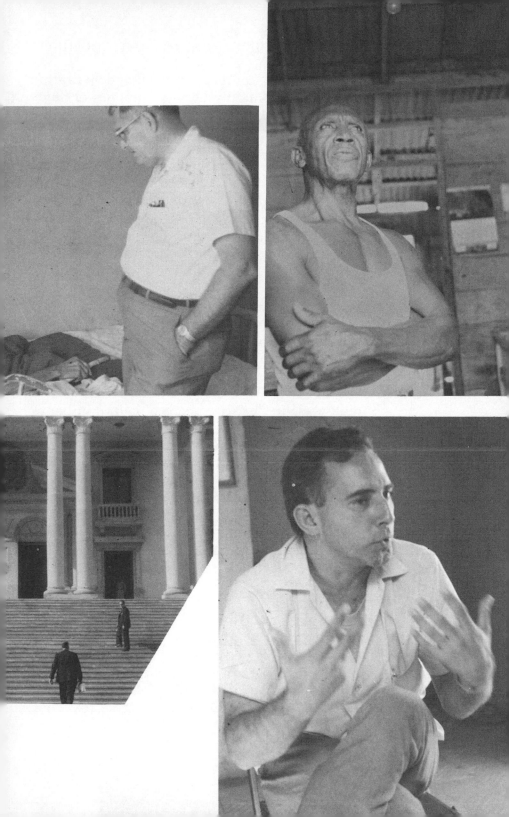

one of the rehydration centers for saving dehydrating babies had shut down—mainly because supplies of fluids and scalp vein kits had become exhausted. During the year the rehydration centers had been in operation, the child death rate from gastroenteritis had dropped six thousand in comparison to the year before. More fluids and kits must now come from MAP, which in turn must get them as gifts from drug companies.

"MAP will help all it can," Howard said (Raymond Knighton, MAP's executive director, concurred), "but it cannot give what it does not have."

Time is required to receive and clear MAP shipments through customs. While I was there eleven tons of MAP medicines and equipment arrived in one shipment. Howard personally had to get exoneration of duty, receive the medicines, have them hauled and stacked in the new MAP warehouse. Jimmy Shoemake keeps records on distribution and receives for the MAP account token sums paid by doctors.

There are now eight Christian medical clinics in Santo Domingo, all supplied by MAP and all begun since Howard's arrival. Three are related to Baptist churches; four are related to other groups; one is the original Christian Medical Society clinic downtown.

Howard is no longer coordinator for the Dominican Christian Medical Society. The majority of Southern Baptist mission members in the D.R. feel that he should restrict his medical work to MAP and Baptist-related institutions. However, he keeps communication wires open with numerous Dominican doctors: evangelical, Catholic, and otherwise.

While I was in the D.R., Howard accepted appointment to the three-member Administrative Committee of the Rehabilitation Center for invalids in Santo Domingo. The only facility for crippled children in the country, it is supported by the Catholic Church, the Alliance for Progress, the United Nations, the Dominican Red Cross, and private individuals. Vivacious, dark-haired Mrs. Mary Marranzini, the Rehab Center's president, said gratefully, "Reverend Shoemake is our best Protestant friend. He is marvelous at persuading other people to help us."

I looked on while Mrs. Marranzini showed Howard a list of medicines needed during the next year. He said simply, "With $400 to pay the freight, we can get them all through MAP. Maybe I can collect some of the money from my friends."

Later we went downtown for some interviews. On the way he stopped at a hardware store on Calle Conde. "The owner is a good Catholic friend," he said as we walked through the door. "I feel impressed to ask him to give some money for the Rehab Center."

The owner greeted us cordially. Howard stated the need for money to pay freight for MAP medicines, and the Dominican gave orders to a clerk. A few moments later she brought a check for $100 and asked what she should put on the voucher. "Just Mr. Shoemake," the man said cordially. "That's enough." Then he added $50 more in cash from his pocket.

As we were leaving the store, Howard said, "He's giving the Bible Society's Christmas story from Luke to ten thousand customers. Another Catholic businessman friend has promised to do the same."

The next day we visited Father Marrero Tomas at his "Tigres Club" in a war-battered police station that had been abandoned during the war. Father Tomas, a Cuban Jesuit, pastors the San Miguel Church which dates from the early sixteenth century. Eight thousand people are in his parish; most of them inhabit an indescribably filthy slum called "The Cave" just behind the church. For organizing street boys and motivating them to build a school for poor children, Father Tomas is called a Communist by a few conservative priests.

The priest remembered Howard. "You brought medicine and food to us during the revolution," he said. "We

Howard Shoemake is still very much involved in medical affairs. *Left,* he talks with nuns about hospital supplies. He serves on the board of the Rehabilitation Center in Santo Domingo. *Below,* he talks to Mrs. Marranzini, the Center's President. *Bottom:* This little girl's braces were supplied through MAP and U.S. AID, with Howard Shoemake's help.

didn't have many friends like you. Many were calling me a 'Communist' because I tried to help the street boys."

Pointing to boys playing in the streets, the priest asked, "Where can they go? What can they do? There is no public swimming pool in the city, no YMCA as you have in the United States. Over there"—he pointed to a barren park—"we could build a 'Y.' It would have a swimming pool, a library, a gymnasium, a shop where boys could learn vocations."

I noticed the priest's shoes were worn and scuffed. On impulse I asked abruptly, "Are those your only shoes, Father?"

The padre looked down and said sadly, "Yes; but how could I have another pair when most of my people have none?"

As we walked away Howard said, "You have to admire him for what he's doing. We're not doing this kind of work."

Late that same afternoon we called on Dr. Orestes Cucurullo, a leading Santo Domingo gynecologist and husband of one of the four doctors baptized in Howard's church.

Dr. Cucurullo is president of the Dominican Association for Family Welfare (Planned Parenthood). He talked enthusiastically about his organization's birth control program, which is tolerated but not officially supported by the Catholic hierarchy. Why did he become involved in birth control? "I felt the misery and the overpopulation of my country." [5] Who supports family planning in the D.R.? "A few brave priests. Church World Service. The

---

[5] The Dominican population is now increasing 3.8 percent per year (births minus deaths). Agricultural production is increasing only 1.5 percent per year. The three largest volunteer agencies in food distribution are CARE, CARITAS (Catholic Charities), and CHURCH WORLD SERVICE (Protestant). Their projections for 1968 are as follows: CARE plans to use 19.9 million pounds of food to feed 348,500 people; CARITAS plans to use 33.9 million pounds to feed 219,000 people; CHURCH WORLD SERVICE plans to use 1.4 million pounds to feed 7,000 people.

Board of Social Action of the Dominican Evangelical Church."

He looked at Howard, who was standing beside me, and said, "I was born a Catholic, but now I sympathize with the Baptists. I know they believe in separation of church and state. They baptize only people who know what they are doing. Since my wife has become an evangelical—a Baptist—life is much better at home."

Howard Shoemake is well aware that the Dominican Republic is bereft of many humanitarian social institutions taken for granted in the U.S. There is no United Fund or Community Chest in Santo Domingo. Charitable organizations must go door to door and beg for support. One businessman said he sometimes received a hundred solicitations in one week.

A Community Chest must have a director who is nonpolitical and is widely trusted and respected. Several Dominicans—businessmen and charity workers—want Howard Shoemake to be that man. But when would he find time?

And there are the students. Going to and fro in the ancient capital, Howard and I frequently drove through the Autonomous University of Santo Domingo. Here—if the news reports are to be believed—is the hotbed of Communist agitation. Off limits to both civil and military authorities, the campus serves as a refuge for political radicals.

There is no full-time evangelical witness to these students. From a Christian student leader, I obtained some facts: About 150 students are evangelicals; half of these are indifferent and uncommitted to Christ. Several cell groups meet daily for Bible study and discussion. Only two evangelical converts have been won during the past two years. Why haven't more students been reached? "The gospel hasn't been presented effectively," the Christian student said.

From various sources I obtained the estimate that there

are only five hundred hard-core Communists among the students, and they are divided between support of the Russian and Chinese systems. The Communists have from two to three thousand sympathizers whom they can count on for demonstrations. Most of the six to seven thousand students are simply indifferent to ideology.

Evangelical students are more popular than those avowedly Catholic. "We feel that evangelicals are more concerned with national conditions than Catholics," one activist student told me.

One day I visited the campus—alone—to sample student opinion. Everywhere I saw pictures and propaganda slogans, almost all pro-Communist and anti-U.S. The portraits of Che Guevera, Mao Tse Tung, Stokely Carmichael, Fidel Castro, Lenin, Marx, and other revolutionaries stared at me from the front of almost every building.

In front of the architecture school, I found a friendly student. As we talked a crowd gathered until I suddenly realized I was surrounded.

A tall, dark-skinned man, about twenty-five, stepped forward and pointed to my camera and tape recorder. "We have been watching you and think you are a C.I.A. agent."

I looked at him and the intense youths that surrounded me. Momentarily I did not know what to say. I felt terribly afraid of violence.

"No, I am only a writer," I said. "I am here to learn from you about the humanitarian needs of your country. I am a free lance. I work for no one." I stressed the last sentence.

The dark-skinned man shot back. "What is your philosophy of life? What do you think about the poverty and misery in our country?"

"I am trying to learn," I said. "As an evangelical, I believe we should do all we can to help the less fortunate."

A low murmur swept through the crowd. I saw several

smiles and sensed there were other evangelicals present.

My accuser raised his hand. "Many of us," he said loudly, "are Marxists and materialists. You evangelicals are well-meaning people, but your dead Christ cannot solve our problems."

I noticed several heads shaking in disagreement. One youth tapped me on the shoulder. "He speaks for himself, not for the rest of us. I believe in Christ."

The dark-skinned man ignored the dissenters and looked squarely at me. "Who is more revolutionary, Christ or Marx? Who has the best program for helping the oppressed masses?"

For the next ninety minutes we debated while the crowd grew even larger. Frequently arguments broke out within the crowd between other students. At last my opponent said, "I must go to class." I thanked him for giving me his views and said, "I must go too." I shook hands with every student in the crowd. They seemed friendly now, even cordial.

Later I mentioned the incident to a U.S. diplomat. "You are lucky to be here," he said drawing a thin smile. "None of us from the embassy would want to go on the campus alone."

Howard was nonchalant when he picked me up in his car. "Why shouldn't you go there?" he asked. "They've always been friendly to me."

He looked at a knot of students and waved. They waved back.

He drove up a hill that overlooked the campus; his face set in thought. "Our generation is not coming up with solutions fast enough to satisfy the desperations of youth," he said again as if he were thinking out loud. "Yes, they are often radical and want today's problems solved yesterday. There may be better ways than what they propose in some situations. But they have compassion in their hearts."

He stopped beside a vacant lot covered with weeds.

"What a beautiful place to build a student center." (I remembered he had said this every time we drove through the campus.) "We need to be here right now witnessing to the students, winning them, harnessing their compassion and concern. They will be the leaders of the future."

I sat beside the tall Texan and looked back toward the campus and the sea that lay beyond. I thought of what I had seen and experienced during the past weeks. How frustrated the missionary must feel, I thought, to see so many needs, to hear so many calls, to stand before so many open doors—and be only one man.

Howard broke into my meditation. "Well, let's get on the hoss and get to the hospital."

We drove to the Robert Reid Cabral Children's Hospital, an imposing, three-story white concrete building overlooking the green sea. Here I met the Director, Dr. Rafael Miranda, a distinguished-looking man who greeted Howard with a comradely embrace. He showed me the room where babies were receiving precious life-giving dextrose. I shuddered at the realization that this was the only place in the country where babies dehydrating from gastroentritis could now receive such infusions.

Dr. Miranda led us on a tour of the hospital. It was clean but sorely lacking in equipment that U.S. hospitals take for granted. Many of the beds were empty. I asked why, in view of the high disease rate in the country.

"Money!" Dr. Miranda explained. "We are supported by the Government with $9,000 a month. This allows us a daily budget of $.27 per bed for food, medicine, and maintenance. But the Government is three months behind with payments to us now."

Howard shrugged. "The Government doesn't have enough money to go around. It's like trying to stretch a handkerchief over a barrel head."

We stopped at a dining room where about forty children were eating soup. I noticed the thin arms, distended

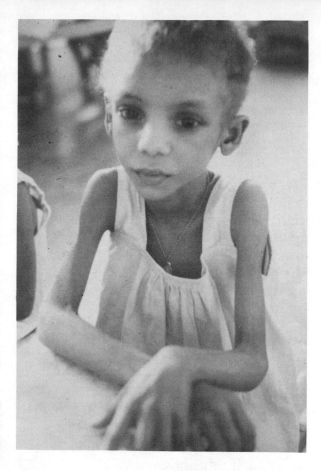

Children like this ten-year-old girl, victims of starvation, are treated at the Robert Reid Cabral Children's Hospital (below). But there is not enough money to equip the hospital properly or to take care of all the children who need help.

stomachs, and pasty skin of several children—sure signs of starvation.

"How old is that child?" I asked the doctor.

"About ten," he said, "and the one beside her is nine."

I shook my head in disbelief. "Neither look any older than my three-year-old Cheryl."

After recovering from this shock, I asked Dr. Miranda how long the children were kept in the hospital.

"We keep some only a few days. Some stay for weeks or months. We have one that has been here six years. Oh, it isn't a question of health. Some parents bring their children here, give wrong addresses, and never return. We can't put them on the streets, so we keep them here. We don't have institutions to care for unwanted children such as you have in the United States."

That evening, a Wednesday, I visited the church in the Union Club for the last time. Dorothy Dell was already there, having come for her earlier Woman's Missionary Union meeting. She reported ten of the fifteen members had been present.

Because Christmas was approaching, Howard led the group of about thirty in singing Christmas carols with his daughter Carol accompanying. Then he projected a Christmas film (from "The Answer" series) on a screen. During quiet spots in the film I could hear the yells of street boys outside.

The dialogue was in Spanish, but the family scenes were North American. More interested in the audience reaction than the film, I watched the Dominican children "ooh" and "ah" at sight of the family in the story riding a sled across a carpet of white snow.

I saw Dr. Cornelio sitting with his arms around two of his three motherless children. The Cornelio boy sat beside Ricky Shoemake. Nearby sat Dra. Gladys Germosen de Mieses, staring entranced at the wintry scenes. I knew that both doctors had spent most of the day treating patients at the medical clinics.

The film ended and Howard announced the hymn, "Joy to the World."

I could not sing for crying. So few Dominicans know this joy.

And I am crying now as I write this last line.

SOURCES AND APPRECIATIONS

My principal resource materials came from over one hundred personal interviews and from impressions gained during my visit to the Dominican Republic.

I thank first the Shoemake family. Howard and Dorothy Dell opened their hearts and confidential files and extended the utmost courtesy and hospitality during my visit to Santo Domingo. Howard cautioned me only to keep the book nonpolitical. He never attempted to dictate an angle or approach.

The Shoemakes' colleagues in the D.R. helped in every way possible and opened their homes and hearts. I thank them.

Dominicans of various occupations and political views helped immensely; some, however, consented to interviews only after they understood the purpose of the book.

These were former and present government officials, doctors, ham operators, housewives, and other patriotic citizens. I thank them all.

J. Raymond Knighton, executive director of MAP, and his Wheaton staff fulfilled every request. Dr. and Mrs. Martin Andrews (Dr. Andrews is a MAP board member) gave valuable assistance

About two dozen evangelical missionaries serving in the D.R. gave me time and information; I thank them.

I express appreciation to many U.S citizens who live now or have lived in the D.R. Lyle Copmann, director of the United States Information Agency in Santo Domingo, and his assistant Franklin Polanco gave me valuable background and their own personal impressions of Howard's works. U.S. State Department personnel in Washington, U.S. AID officials and technicians in the D.R., Peace Corpsmen in the D.R., US military personnel at Fort Bragg, the Penick Gentrys, and many others were helpful.

About half of the photographs appearing in the book were selected from the hundreds of pictures I took in the D.R. The Shoemake family pictures are from their files. The military photographs were supplied by the United States Information Agency in Santo Domingo. A few pictures were provided by Medical Assistance Programs.

There are few good books in print that help in understanding the land Columbus "loved most." A modern history of the D.R. remains to be written. There have been, however, numerous magazine articles and news reports published since the 1965 revolution. *Time* magazine's reports are perhaps the best and least biased and were helpful to me.

For readers interested in exploring the Dominican Republic in greater depth, I suggest these books:

Trujillo. Robert D. Crassweller, New York: The Macmillan Co., 1966. (No one can understand the D.R. without studying the man Trujillo and his tragic thirty-year rape of the nation. This is the best biography of the dictator in print.)

Overtaken by Events, John Bartlow Martin, Garden City, New York: Doubleday & Co., Inc., 1966. (Martin, a brilliant writer on social issues, was President Kennedy's ambassador to the D.R. from 1962 to 1964, when he resigned to write this lengthy 821-page book. No one has done a better job of exposing the problems of the country as it struggles toward an uncertain future.)

Revolt of the Damned, Dan Kurzman, New York: Van Rees Press, 1965. (Written by a veteran foreign correspondent, the book is critical of U.S. involvement in the 1965 crisis.)

The Unfinished Experiment, Juan Bosch, New York: Frederick A. Praeger, 1965. (The controversial Dominican ex-President, who remains a strong influence in the country, recounts his own views and attempts to help the country emerge into mature nationhood.)

The Church and the Crisis in the Dominican Republic, Fr. James A. Clark, Westminster, Maryland: The Newman Press. (Though poorly organized and written, the author presents some insights into Catholic problems in the D.R. and the deep divisions within the church over solutions.)

Dominican Action—1965: Intervention or Cooperation? The Center for Strategic Studies, Washington, D.C.: Georgetown University, 1966. (An objective day-by-day reporting of the events in April and early May that shook the hemisphere.)

Area Handbook for the Dominican Republic, Washington, D.C.: Foreign Area Studies, The American University, 1966. (The best up-to-date compilation of basic facts about the social, economic, political, military institutions and practices of the D.R. Secure as No. 550.54 for $2.25 from the Superintendent of Documents, U.S. Government Printing Office, Washington, D.C. 20402.)

Finally, I express thanks to those who contributed to the actual preparation of the manuscript:

My wife, Marty, patiently endured my absence from home while doing research and worked with me on revision of the rough draft and correcting of the galleys.

Mrs. Paula Kelly did her usual superb job of typing the publisher's manuscript.

Howard and Dorothy Dell Shoemake and J. Raymond Knighton read the entire manuscript and made factual corrections. A few other people read portions which related to their special knowledge.

It is not trite to say that I thank God for giving me the opportunity to transmit this story to what is hoped will be a host of readers. Through His providence and direction I met Howard Shoemake, and by His strength and guidance I was able to finish the book, imperfect though it is.

ARLINGTON HEIGHTS, ILLINOIS
June 1, 1968

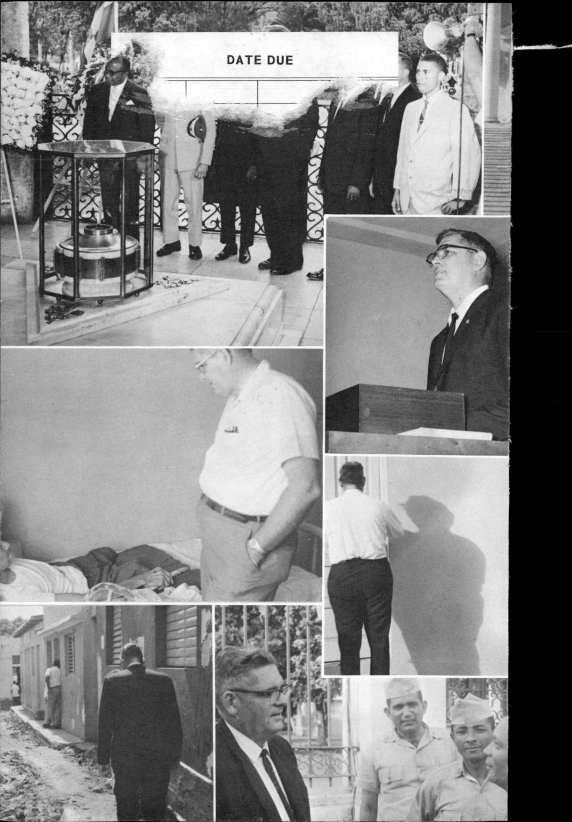

DATE DUE